TRUTH, BEAUTY
and GOODNESS

the future of education,
healing arts and health care

Michaela Glöckler, MD

Printed with support from the Waldorf Curriculum Fund

Published by:

Waldorf Publications at the
Research Institute for Waldorf Education
351 Fairview Avenue, Suite 625
Hudson, NY 12534

TRUTH, BEAUTY and GOODNESS

The future of education, healing arts and health care

Michaela Glöckler, MD

Four lectures and subsequent written additions, edited from the Hawai'i International Health and Education Kolisko Conference, Honolulu Waldorf School, February, 2018.

© Michaela Glöckler, MD, 2018, 2019

Editor and publisher: C. Neil Carter, **m.g.tbg18@gmail.com**

Acknowledgments and many thanks to those who gave editorial assistance; for support from Van James, Bonnie Ozaki-James and all the team of Conference organizers' and staff at the Honolulu Waldorf School, the Anthroposophical Society in Hawai'i, Paul LeGrand and Dr Jocelyn Romero Demirbag for use of video and notes, and to New Zealand colleagues, especially Neil Boland for his assistance formatting references.

Permissions: Van James for drawings from his book, *Drawing with Hand, Head and Heart*, and also Iris Sullivan, workshop participant, for the pastel of the conference theme for the front cover of this book.

First printing 2018 by Angus Donaldson Copy Service, Christchurch, NZ
Original ISBN assigned through the
New Zealand National Library

Second printing 2019 by Waldorf Publications
ISBN# 978-1-943582-32-7

PREFACE

Dear Readers,

In September 2019, Waldorf/Rudolf Steiner Education will celebrate its centenary. Starting with the first school in Stuttgart,Germany, this approach to teaching is now found in more than a thousand schools and five thousand kindergartens worldwide, almost all initiated by parents looking for new pedagogical pathways. As an education which is not primarily based on expectations from society and business life, the Waldorf approach consequently follows the question: What does the human being need in the years of growth and mental development in order that it may develop most healthily? What is the age-appropriate content of learning to best stimulate the development of body soul and spirit? Following such a new direction, the three classic ideals of humanity known as Truth, Beauty and Goodness play a significant role for teachers and parents in the companionship of the children and youngsters. Why? They express true humanity!

Truth, Beauty and Goodness belong to some of the most valuable experiences in the whole course of our life. Moments of truth, of genuine understanding, lead us toward enduring and trustworthy human encounters. We require beauty in order to live. If we cannot find life beautiful, then we cannot really live. Life is full of contradictions. We are born, we die, we breathe in and we breathe out, we can react with both love and with hatred. We have to learn to find ourselves in our encounters with these contradictions. By finding life's beauty, we learn to recognize that we can learn from everything that happens and that there is no light without its shadows. Striving in the pursuit of the Good, however, is the foundation of morality and ethics. Meeting a 'good' person is a gift of destiny. A good human being is able to separate from their selves and have the presence of mind to do what is fitting to the moment and be of immediate use.

In Waldorf education, these truly human, basic ideals are of the highest value, not only for the self-education of the teacher, but also for the understanding of development in childhood and youth. High standards of truthfulness and accuracy are required for thinking and observation skills. The development of a healthy feeling life requires differentiation between the beautiful and the ugly in such a form that the youngster learns to develop sympathy for the beautiful and antipathy for what is destructive or ugly. In contrast, the education of the will requires a gesture of independence from the other but also the capacity for a person to distance themselves from their own needs and instead to be in the position to help and give to others what they need.

From my heart I wish to thank the colleagues of the Honolulu Waldorf School and the Anthroposophical Society in Hawai'i most warmly for their invitation to the Kolisko Conference 2018, to speak on this theme from the basis of my experience as a pediatrician and Waldorf school doctor in Germany. Also, I wish to thank the editor and publisher, Neil Carter, for bringing my lecture transcriptions, references, and my subsequent written additions into good English. May this book be a contribution, especially in the light of today's increasing digitalization, to help set a new standard to benefit the development of children and youth. May these ideals of truth, beauty and goodness become our guiding stars in a world in need of more humanity.

– Michaela Glöckler, MD
Goetheanum, Dornach, Switzerland

1: TRUTH

Aloha! Good morning, dear friends,

I am glad that here, in Hawai'i, the center of the Pacific, we can take the time to focus on truth, beauty and goodness and their relevance to our everyday teaching and working with children and youth. I begin with words by Rudolf Steiner which are not so easy to understand; they come from the year 1919, made some months after the foundation of the Waldorf School. He points out that, in the middle of the 20th century, humanity would more and more experience 'burn out' phenomena:

*Those forces of humanity's evolution which have so far guided man unconsciously, so that he has been able to advance, are becoming exhausted and will be entirely exhausted by approximately the middle of the century. **The new forces must be drawn from depths of souls; and man must come to understand that in the depths of his soul he is connected with the roots of spiritual life.**[1]*

Looking back into the past, Rudolf Steiner describes how mankind's development was still guided by the wisdom of the ancient mysteries and great leaders of humanity. From the 15th century on, humans became more and more independent from spiritual and political authorities and more ready to find the sources of strength and guidance within themselves. Therefore education must support this process of individualization and finding inner spiritual guidance through one's true spiritual self. Without this new resource of inner strength, humans will not be able to remain healthy throughout their lives. In the Waldorf School foundation course,[2] Steiner

1 Steiner, R. (1919/1945). *The mission of light, of space and of the Earth* (F.E. Dawson, trans.) [GA 194, lecture 3]. New York, NY: Anthroposophical Press.
2 Steiner, R. (1919/1996). *The foundations of human experience* (R.F. Lathe, trans.) [GA 293, lecture 1]. Great Barrington, MA: Anthroposophic Press.

develops the perspective of an education not build on egoism, the shadow side of Materialism, which arose from the 15th century onward.

On a daily basis, we read much about environmental influences which are damaging to our health. These influences are well known as the shadow sides of a way of thinking which reduces the evolution of earth and humans to the material. How can the educational environment be organized in such a way that a compensation for this one-sidedness can come about? From life experience we learn that it is only when we have lost something that the full appreciation can be felt of just how valuable it was. Then we invest a lot of energy to find ways for finding it again or how to re-establish it in a new form. The signature of our present period of time can be seen in this perspective. Maybe a lot of things in different fields of life have to develop so destructively in order that as many people as possible will wake up and realize that human life and its values, dignity and health must be viewed anew.

The more we lose our health, the more we appreciate it and are aware that we need to do something about it. In the same way, we face much more awareness today for what is true, beautiful and good because we are missing it. In this context it is exciting how many initiatives are emerging today for the protection of the environment, for caring for plants and animals, being aware of the global destruction on our planet and climate problems. Exciting too are those activities which strive to practice ethical banking, business and leadership. New trademarks and brands are developing based on their moral stance and with guarantees that they are free of corrupt practices and egocentrism. We appreciate such impulses. But we still do not ask consequentially enough for an ethical education, which can empower the necessary human capacities to meet the problems of our time. We encounter many children who have been severely affected by the media, by being neglected, or by their materialistic life circumstances. If they do not get the chance to meet educators with an empathic healing orientation, they may be endangered for their entire biography.

People like me, when invited to speak in Waldorf schools in Europe, are frequently asked to talk about teachers' health and strength and how they may cope with the many changes in the teaching profession today. We face an environment with increasing demands and requirements from bureaucracy. We experience symptoms of 'burn out' and the challenge of a generation of children who are more and more difficult to handle. You will know best about the situation in your own school, but one common lack I have noticed is that the adults are not sufficiently able to form a strong working community in their schools that is built on trust and mutual support and also on individual initiative. We have on our Waldorf banner, *Education toward Freedom, toward Individualism.* However, it can happen, for example, that when we are sitting together in a Faculty meeting of teachers, if one of us is exhausted, then an unhelpful response might be, 'Why are you so exhausted? Look at me; I did this and this and this!' We start to compare and hence lose our sense for the individuality. Amongst adults, there is much that we can improve in regards to being honest and showing real interest in the other's situation.

Talking to you like this appears demanding, but to speak about truth, beauty and goodness is even more so. However, these three ideals have a basic human side to them which everyone can understand and start to work with. That is because these virtues are not just purely academic ones (which can fill whole libraries). Rather, they penetrate much further into basic human values, which, when they fail or are missing, cause so many illnesses, whereas, when they are present, they enhance our health. Just as human relationships are poisoned and disturbed through untruthfulness, ugliness and evil deeds, so we can find healing in all our efforts, no matter how small, in trying to be honest and harmonious, in striving to look for what is the needed good in a certain situation. These three superhuman capabilities are closely related.

But: Truth, beauty and goodness resonate with each other. Beauty is one of the biggest symbols of our time. All the young people have their own sense for beauty and want to appear as beautiful as possible. But what is the characteristic of beauty? It seems easier to approach truth than to approach beauty or goodness. Beauty appears to be very individual. We have a proverb in German, which roughly corresponds in English to 'Beauty is in the eye of the beholder,' as each one of us has their own aesthetic judgment. There are no general characteristics of what is beautiful or not. It's a matter of 'like or not like.' Truth, beauty and goodness resonate with each other. Beauty without truth or goodness is not beauty; truth without beauty and goodness is not really truth and, what is goodness without truth and beauty?

We may associate **truth** with thinking and observation, beauty with our feeling life and goodness with our will. The biggest mystery however, is that of the 'I,' the human 'I am.' It is the 'I' which looks for truth and has a longing for beauty and goodness.

Those who are looking for truth have to go alone...
— Christian Morgenstern

If you are a teacher and you have a certain number of students, then, it is possible that each one of those students will have a different approach to understand something.

That means the teacher has to work hard to find how to help each one to find their own path! Truth is in the middle. I learned about this during my first practical as a school doctor in a school. While observing in a classroom, I noticed that some children 'tuned out,' became sleepy, or were distracted during lessons. I observed that

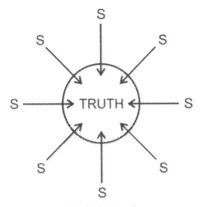

Fig 1.1 Truth

it is not the rule that all the students can really follow the whole teaching! I asked my husband, Georg, who was a math teacher, "How did you manage in math lessons, as according to the statistics, about forty percent of students become drop outs in math? What really is teaching and how do you reach all the students?"

My husband replied, "I had a wonderful introduction to good Waldorf education when I had my first Waldorf block of lessons as a young math teacher. Coming freshly from my academic education, I introduced algebra. The ninth grade class students had to understand that a + b = c. That is not so easy to understand. I asked my students, who got it? Quite a number raised their hand but many did not. I explained again, and asked them the other way round, Who did not yet understand? Many raised their hands! I explained a third time, asked again and almost the same number of hands went up. What was I to do?[3] Before I tried to explain a fourth time, one girl helped me. She said, 'But Mr Glöckler, you explained each of the three times the same way!' I understood how silly this was. That was my most powerful lesson in didactics."

---

3 German proverb, 'Wie ein begossener Pudel' (*Like a drenched poodle*).

Each child has the right to meet the truth upon their own pathway. If a teacher thinks that if other people must take the same road to understanding as they themselves do, then that teacher has not understood about truth. A teacher is certainly lucky if just one third of the class can follow. The next step is to make the teaching accessible to the rest of the group. In those early days, we had a five and a half day teaching week (i.e., school was also held on Saturday mornings), so because he was teaching the 9th grade on the Saturday morning, my husband invited those students who did not understand to bring him questions during the Saturday afternoon. In that way, the students helped him become a more sensitive teacher. We can only learn from the children how to help them to find their ways. We cannot 'know' it, nor can we can learn it from books. We can only, as Steiner recommended, read the children's needs. For this, we need to open our eyes and find the will and the courage to see truth—the truth of each child. We need to observe the way the child's thoughts and feelings can be mobilized, how skillful they are and what makes them active.

A 'horror' subject, like math, was transformed into a subject of success, which the children really liked. For me, as a young, inexperienced school doctor, this was very impressive. This eye opener helped me to see the importance of the teacher/student interaction. If this interaction is harmonious, orientated toward truth, beauty and a foundation of goodwill, then the children will feel that the teacher wishes to help and to understand them.

The first step of truth finding – observation

How can we find and teach the truth and how can we access truth in our normal, everyday life? When I first studied the Waldorf curriculum, I wondered why Rudolf Steiner wanted us to ask children as early as grade one such questions as, "What did you observe on your way to school or what was a new experience for you yesterday?" If the children tell the teacher about something new, then Steiner suggested that we continue, "How did this person look, what color clothes did this person wear?" By this means we train clear memory and good observation for what was said and also for how it was expressed. For example, if you ask students (especially those whose parents have also asked such questions at home) about what the teacher or the students wore, then you will find that the children have observed exactly, and they can tell you all about the colors and the fashion. Rudolf Steiner wanted teachers to train good observation from the first school day on. The better I can observe, the more clearly I can say, "Yes, that is so." Thinking and good observation are the basic tools to find truth.

This morning I was given wonderful lei of Hawaiian flowers to wear around my neck. [The audience were shown the lei]. It is made from beautiful, natural plants and blue flowers. If you now close your eyes, you can make a more or less clear picture of what it is. Within a week, the actual lei and its fresh beauty will have disappeared. However, in your imagination, it will still be as fresh as it was on the first day. When, each evening, we review our day, we can re-live our observations and experiences and see them again in our mind. We bring what we have seen in the environment into the invisible realm of thinking. We give something which has gone and will eventually die (as does everything in the world of the senses), eternal life in our thoughts.

Observations, using our senses as transmitters, are essential and fundamental for our relationship to our physical environment for schooling. Schooling the senses has become the newest essential for 'truth education.' A major effect of the media has been to attack our ability to school our senses and our ability to find the truth and the good. The present generation of children are already the third 'screen generation.' The first screen generation came from the general public availability of television. The second generation were exposed to all the channels being open for twenty-four hours a day, so the effect was greatly intensified. Nowadays, with the third generation, everything is available instantly on mobiles, kept in your pocket or even when driving in a car.

Wishes and intentions to come to our own individual experiences can be totally suppressed by 'pre-formed inputs,' so we become 'mass human beings,' sharing the same images with millions. These pictures are not truth, they are not real, neither are their colors or forms. The sense impressions come only through our eyes and ears, so if we touch the images on the screen, the touch experience is always the same and has nothing to do with the experience were we to touch the real object. Our senses become disintegrated. The media becomes a huge 'sensory disintegration machine,' which suppresses our will to observe for ourselves. Many parents can be unaware of what their children are missing because the parents themselves missed out.

If we want to do something for truth education, we really need to make our kindergartens and schools strictly media- and screen-free.[4] Our schools and kindergartens have a huge responsibility not only toward each child's development but also the added responsibility to make parents aware of the reasons.

The etheric organization of the human being and the second step of truth finding

One of Steiner's greatest findings was his discovery that forces of growth metamorphose into intellectual forces. The same forces which make your body grow, regenerate and gain health, the so called Self-healing forces, are the same forces which are appearing gradually as the forces of our thinking capacity; our life of thoughts. What lets

---

4 www.eliant.eu-European Alliance of Initiatives for Applied Anthroposophy; R. Brinton & M. Glöckler (Eds.). (2019). *Growing up healthy in a world of digital media: A guide for parents and caregivers of children and adolescents* (A. Klee, Trans.). Stroud, UK: InterActions.

our body grow is the same capacity which is manifesting in another form by serving our spiritual growth, mental healing and health. This insight can help us to understand why meditative pathways, good thoughts and prayers for other people can support their state of health. This is because the etheric is the same sheath, serving both thinking and life. This law is fundamental for both anthroposophic medicine and education. We can readily observe, year by year in the first twenty years of life, how, as the body grows, the more new intellectual faculties appear, ready for thinking and learning.

A well-known example of the above that Steiner often refers to is the second dentition as a marker for school readiness and the development of abstract memory. Between six and eight years old, most children can accurately recall the teacher's words from the day before, even if they have heard them only once. In my medical studies, I learned how the second dentition is all prepared in the mandibular and maxilla, even though the second teeth are not all broken through in the mouth.[5] As a young school doctor during my practical placements, I observed on several occasions in first grade classes what happened after a teacher had announced to their children that they were to hear this or that fairy tale. If it was a story that the children had already heard the previous year in kindergarten, I could especially see the different stages of maturity within those classes of children. Some children were happy to hear the beautiful story again, as they were not yet at the stage of using abstract memory (their memory lives still in repetition, like a kindergarten child). However, those who were school-ready and already developing their abstract memory said, "Oh, that's boring. Why that old story?" They were annoyed! And then there would be a middle group, neither excited

---

5 Hoffmeister H. (1989). Development, decay, changing of teeth and malposition of teeth and jaw. In D.S. Mitchell (Ed.) *Developmental insights: Discussions between doctors and teachers* (pp.51–94). Longmont, CO: AWSNA. A compendium of lectures from the first Kolisko Conference, Stuttgart, November, 1989.

nor annoyed but just behaving politely. Steiner wanted us to observe such interrelationships between the maturation process of the body and the appearance of the corresponding intellectual capacities.

Etheric forces first have to make the body develop. But when this is done, these forces begin gradually to be liberated, and then they become the carrier of our thinking development. Etheric forces continuously liberate from birth as long we are growing. Each year, new intellectual processes develop, depending upon the organs being formed. For Steiner, teeth changes are such a beautiful example, as teeth do not regenerate nor prepared for a third dentition. We all know what that means: 'More money for the dentist!' With no chance for further regeneration, all the etheric forces that went into the second dentition begin to be liberated. We then develop the 'spiritual bite' (i.e., we can 'chew over' or 'get our teeth into' something), which is the faculty of abstract thinking. If we have heard something, we can memorize it independently of space and time. Abstract thinking means that it is independent from where it came. Steiner's advice was that teachers should school the children's intellectual faculties in the first school years by accompanying the introduction of reading and writing with skillful physical activity, artistic work, handcraft and harmonious movements. The more the growing body is educated, the better will be its maturation and the quality of later thinking capacities. Formal sports should only start in the middle grades, around grade four, because these movements are more mechanical, i.e., less 'living.' In Steiner's time it was believed that the brain developed out of its genetic predisposition. Today we know the brain is an organ which can develop only in the encounter with the physical environment in time and space. If these experiences are not skillful, if the body doesn't have a good space orientation, and if thinking and feeling have no clear contact with time processes, then thinking and observation are not rooted in reality. Children would then have no clear mental orientation. Brain development would be damaged.

As we age, each organ liberates etheric forces and, as skin may also be considered an organ, we become 'wiser' but less 'beautiful'! The greatest 'mental beauty' we have in life will be when all our forces are liberated, when we leave our physical body and enter into our spiritual journey after death. It is the etheric invisible body, which is the carrier of life on earth and of our 'eternal' life in thoughts within the spiritual world.[6] In *Foundations of Human Experience*[7] (the first course of the lectures to teachers of the first Waldorf School), Steiner describes how the etheric organization builds the bridge between the outer environment and our sense perceptions. In the evening, our senses are tired. It is the same with the brain. In the evening our head is tired. All the other organs apart from the brain and sense organs do not need to sleep. Mental activity is an 'organ abusing activity,' a tiring, destructive activity. Our spiritual awareness is the result of an 'out of body' activity of our etheric constitution. In sleep we do not think, because the entire the etheric forces are engaged to regenerate brain and sense organs.

Most of our thoughts are related to observations of our senses. They are 'representations' of sense experiences. When we go beyond this way of thinking merely in mental representations and images, we come to true thinking, which is independent of our mental representations. That is the second step of truth finding, when we think with our etheric body independently from our sense impressions. That is what we name philosophy: Thinking in concepts, principles, logic and relationships. For example, thinking in mathematical terms in geometry, the definition of a circle is not simply the drawing of a circle in this figure:

---

6 Steiner, R. (1912-13/1978). *Life between death and rebirth* (R.M. Querido, trans.) [GA 140]. London: Anthroposophical Press.

7 Steiner, R. (1919/1996). *The foundations of human experience* (R.F. Lathe, trans.) [GA 293]. Great Barrington, MA: Anthroposophic Press.

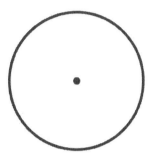

Fig. 1.2 Circle and point

Rather, the definition of a circle is: The location [locus] of all the numerous points that have the same distance from the middle point. Such a definition is independent of sense perceptions. I can have a very small circle and central point in mind, or I can make it as large as the cosmos. It is independent of space and sense perception. Our thinking can enter into this space, via the doorways of the senses, and can also leave it and enter the beautiful realm of pure, clear, thinking, independent of sense perception related to space and time. This has to be trained in schools in our times because materialistic academic studies and their resulting curricula demand that every thought be based on [visible] facts. The second step of truth finding is based on thinking, through logic, mathematics and philosophy. Rudolf Steiner's doctoral thesis can be traced in his book, *Philosophy of Freedom*.[8] He wanted to have more time to write another version of his thesis for young people, and he later said, "Each youngster should learn to write their own *Philosophy of Freedom*."[9]

8 Steiner, R. (1893/1999). *Philosophy of freedom*. London: Rudolf Steiner Press. Latest English translation published as: Steiner, R. (1894/1995). *Intuitive thinking as a spiritual path* (M. Lipson, trans., centennial ed.) [GA 4]. Hudson, NY: Anthroposophic Press.
9 Wember, V. (1991). *The will to be free: A philosophy for young people*. London: Temple Lodge Publishing.

With these two steps, we can really educate in school: by caring how we work with the Waldorf curriculum and by thinking how we can help children to remember by using careful observation, mental representation and characterizing things. Waldorf education is a healthy education. This reminds me of an encounter I had yesterday in a shoe shop near here. I said to the man serving, "You are doing a good job; you are so friendly with the customers." He really was, so I told him that I was not on holiday, but working in the nearby Waldorf school. I asked him if he knew the Honolulu Waldorf School. He replied, "Yes, that is a well-known school in the department here; they do many things differently, as they are a school of alternative education." When I asked if he knew what sort of alternative education, he replied. "No, but I would love to know." I replied, "For me, the biggest difference between the regular school system and the Waldorf school is that their alternative is *to orient the education to the developmental needs of the children rather than to the political and economic requirements of society*. It was so nice how this gentleman radiated in agreement.

The third step toward truth finding and the astral forces of feeling

The first two steps of truth finding are safe and clear. Facts are facts, no doubt. Mathematical laws are crystal clear. Their wisdom has an eternal character. But the third and fourth level of finding and approaching truth are different. There is a sphere of truth you can only strive for but you will never find it. Why is this so? Facts are not everything! When people ask me about Waldorf education and I share that it is a 'health promoting education,' mostly they ask me back, "What is your reference?" Rather than wanting to understand or to think conceptually about the development of education, they want just facts and information. Laziness in thinking is already so powerful in materialistic times that we believe only what is based on facts. That means other dimensions of looking for truth are left aside.

However, facts are changing permanently according to the latest news and research. Quite recently, we even have 'fake news' as part of our truth finding facts! We now have to judge what we hear: Is it based on facts which can show the truth or is this fake news, based on facts nicely dressed up to show what I want to find or to explain to you as the truth? It can be convention, intention or manipulation, a mere tool which can be handled to whatever purpose is required. This is the result of a materialistic education and academic training, based only on facts and not on true thoughts. When thinking serves only the observation, then it will lose its own dignity, self-awareness and capacity.

Thinking and observation must be trained and developed in the first seven years of schooling (7–14 years) primarily. This is crucial. Once the astral forces are liberated from their work in the body in the process of puberty, then they are freed for feeling as the life forces of the etheric for thinking. Steiner is using the word *astral* for the 'carrier of our soul forces based on feelings,' because the stars (Latin: *aster*) are connected with the spiritual homeland of our souls, which is why we love the stars so much. These forces relate to the activities of differentiation in our body, for example, cell differentiation leading to gender differentiation. When children in puberty start to live fully in their feelings and not any more like pre-puberty children, living still more in thoughts and observations , then their thought life must have been educated in the years beforehand, so that there is a foundation and support when waves of feelings overwhelm them and make them dream and think in another way.

Doubts, experiences, and their interpretations are based on personal feelings. After teenagers have conversed, they then endlessly reflect if what they have heard is really true. They can feel afterward that what they have said has been misunderstood. The sense for truth is lost when truth is kept only at the level of feelings. Observation skills are lost if you are thinking to interpret your feelings and have to explain them to others. Without clear thoughts and observations based on a fundament of truth, then the sense for truth is endangered. A state of chaos is reached where everything is relative. Instead of knowing, there comes a period of longing, wishing, doubting and insecurity, based upon individual feelings which are still in need of developing. Students of this age are in danger of losing their trust in life, friendship, love, even trust in their parents and themselves.

We need to bear in mind that to meet truth on the astral, emotional level, then truth needs to become a goal and not something we can find here and now. Gotthold Lessing, a German philosopher in the time of the French Revolution, when thinking was a highest virtue, describes the education of humanity and he closed with the following, beautiful parable:

If God would ask me, 'What do you want? Here in my right hand I have all the truth of the world. I am ready to give it to you. Here in my left hand, I have the eternal striving for truth. You will never fully reach it. Which would you like to choose?' Then I would go on my knees, fall in his left hand and say, 'Give me those truths which I can eternally strive for, because the full truth is only for you.'

When I first read this, as a teenager in my Waldorf school time, I thought I would have chosen the other way round. I would have asked for the right hand to save so much suffering! But, as I grew older, I realized that Lessing is right. I would rather follow Lessing's decision. Why? Imagine you would have everything you can learn as a human being right away. You would be at the end of your development, at a dead end. The other way is to experience your astral body as the 'body of becoming,' of becoming a true, individual human being. We are all individuals because of our feelings. On the other hand, we are not individuals because of our physical and etheric forces. Each of us has our own way toward truth and an individual relationship with facts. Some facts in research speak to me strongly, and for other people, not.

They are attracted by other results of this or that finding. What makes us individuals is our destiny, woven out of all the many relationships based upon feelings. Our individualization process is based neither on heredity nor on environment. For example, identical twins share the same hereditary substance and environment, yet they have their individual destiny and partners. Our individuality is based primarily on our individual destiny experience via our astral body, giving us individual consciousness and the power of feeling. Goethe said, "If you don't feel it, you will never understand it." Rudolf Steiner relates that it is through our feelings that thoughts and concepts become relevant for us. If you don't feel the beauty on the inside, if it's not relevant for you, it will pass you by.[10]

Under the aspect of truth, we need to understand that on the astral level, truth is a goal. Truth is something we are longing for, a real self-understanding. Who am I as a human being? Who is really the other person with whom I am living in friendship or with whom I am working? We never reach the end because we are all in development and changing. Our consciousness is changing. That is the astral quality of truth. The more we have interest for one another, the more we understand us in our changing developmental needs. I have observed students in their last years of schooling beginning to reflect, "Shall we not also write an annual report about our teachers?!" Then they write how Mr so and so, gym teacher or handcraft teacher or whoever, "has developed quite nicely this year; he has managed and now knows better how to handle a particular student. We acknowledge that brave soul, go ahead like this!" It is not only we, who as teachers write reports. Students also see our changes on the astral level.

---

10 Steiner, R. (1910/1994). *Theosophy: An introduction to the spiritual processes in human life and in the cosmos* (C. Creeger, trans.) [GA 9]. Hudson, NY: Anthroposophic Press.

The fourth step – Truth at the level of the 'I-organization'

We have considered Truth from the levels of physical, etheric and astral. Now, the fourth level:

- Physical organization—observations, mental representations and concepts

- Etheric organization—mathematical and pure philosophical concepts

- Astral organization—truth becomes something to strive for. What we find true is changing through our life experiences, influenced by our wishes desires and hopes.

- 'I-organization'—truth becomes an ideal, an eternal entity, drawn out of the spiritual world.

What is an ideal? Ideals are drawn out of the spiritual world and are transformed into thoughts. When Christ says in the Gospels, "I am the truth" or "I am the path, the truth and the life," He is relating His being with a thought. If we do not take it to heart, this thought, for us as humans, is a simple thought. It becomes an exceptional and powerful thought only when we identify with it. Ideals are thoughts that have their meaning only in the power of identification. If an idea is not an ideal, then it is still a simple idea, a nice concept. For example, "It's good if people are true. That's a very nice thought, but it has nothing to do with me." However, if this idea, this concept, touches us and we feel a call that we should become more truthful, we might think further, "Maybe I should train my honesty a bit." Honesty then becomes a human faculty that is more than a thought.

Thinking a thought is a bridge between the world of the senses and the world of the spiritual beings. The specific quality of an ideal is that I connect with the being behind or 'within' that thought. If we identify with a good thought, such as an ideal like truth, then the being of truth, the Godhood itself, can strengthen us because we identify with the force of that being. If people train the ideal of honesty, then one day, someone in their environment will see that and say, "Wow, you are honest." Firstly, you thought honesty, next you thought, "There is more, I want to become more honest." Thirdly, honesty might become your ideal, and as a fourth step, you experience this ideal in your daily practice. It gives you strength, enlivens and inspires you, so that in certain situations, you are more honest than you were before. You become as a being which previously was only a thought. There you have a bridge between the outer and inner world, the superficial world and the essential world.

That is one pathway to finding truth through all the four levels of our existence. Waldorf education wants to leave the students free, and the more we understand these different levels of truth, the better we can use the tools of our curriculum to help the students to become oriented and sure on these different levels for their personal truth finding.

A medical viewpoint[11]

From the medical side, truth is a most important concept for all those who want to work with healing, transformation and health support. Health is not the opposite of illness. Illness is an attack on our health. Every day we have to suffer lots of influences that make us ill. These can come from the environment, such as poisoned air, a contaminated or insufficient water supply, nutrition or also emotional problems. We can live in relationships which make us ill. So many factors are playing out. Illness can lead to auto-aggression or to our hating ourselves and our destiny. Self-harm and self-hate are also forces which undermine our health. Forces of healing, self-healing, can compensate for what

---

11 Glöckler, M., Langhammer, S., Wiechert, C. (2006). *Education: Health for life.* Dornach, CH: Anthroposophic Medicine Foundation & Medical Section of the Goetheanum.

we have lost. The so called 'healthy human being' is in the middle, between healing and attacking sources. You do not have two hours in your life in the same state of health. Your health is permanently changing and you are as healthy as you feel yourself to be. There are no objective criteria for what constitutes a healthy or an unhealthy human being; it is an individual balance between patho-genic and saluto-genic influences.

In the 1970s and 80s, I met with a retired anthroposophic actor, who used to visit Waldorf schools to give classes in drama and speech formation. I was present as the school doctor in one of these courses. Teachers were interested to use the tools of speech formation for health promotion. One teacher wanted a speech exercise to help them become stronger, another wanted to be more audible; there were many wishes. It all became a bit much for the speech teacher and she broke out in Swabian[12] dialect, "You know, you don't need to be so enormously healthy, in order to appear healthy!" Of course, she was right, as it depends so much on how you handle your state of health. It's an everyday experience in medical practice that patients can already feel better once they arrive at the hospital or consultation room. Even symptoms can disappear once the doctor arrives! This happens because we relax and can feel, "Now I am helped." Fear disappears and the astral body can liberate itself from the physical. You feel better and your body is thankful. We can also do this consciously, out of our own understanding. We have resources for health on all levels: physical, etheric, astral and I-organization.

It is the etheric body which is the regulator of all these forces, via the four ethers[13] (physical via life ether, etheric via chemical ether, astral

12 German: *Wiessen Sie, Sie brauchen gar nicht so gesund sein, um gesund zu wirken!*

13 Marti, E. (2017). *The etheric: Broadening science through anthroposophy– Volume 1: The world of the ethers* (P. King, trans.). Forest Row, UK: Temple Lodge Publishing.

via light ether, and I-organization via the warmth ether). The etheric body is the health promoter in our body. It is the organization with which we think, it is the carrier of truth and, in that way, health and truth are the same. Health is a wonderful resonance between all the organs. Each organ has a clear perception of the state of activity of all the others and is constantly adjusting to them.

You see the physician only if something is wrong with you. When we become ill, there is a lack of resonance between the organs and the inter-organic communication between cells in the organs. The whole working of all the organs, coordinated by heart and brain in a harmonious healthy interaction, becomes disturbed. We can then understand why we can influence our state of health, not only through remedies but also through meditative pathways. The same members, active in our thinking, feeling and observing are the same ones which have to be regulated in our body in order to keep us healthy.

Day and night learning and truth

The threefold human being in us works differently depending upon whether we are awake or asleep. For the day life, truth has a certain perspective, emotionally and in the way we think, observe and interpret. This, of course, depends upon our own viewpoint. During the night we experience the truth of the others in an unconscious way. Were we conscious of other person's truths, it would be most disturbing! But sometimes, upon waking, we might experience a 'resonance' that maybe we should not press the send button of an email we took time to write the previous day! We might instead think that we should personally contact this person to whom we had written. During sleep, our visions and opinions have slightly changed, and we then look at some things differently. This we can call Night Teaching.

We need the night so that what we learned during the day becomes organic and memorable and can become a faculty. We need the night as well to experience the full truth: During the day we experience our own aspect of truth, as to how we liked, thought or experienced it. During sleep we experience the other half of truth, namely, what other people experienced in meeting and interacting with us. But there is a third strand which, for teachers and parents, is important to know. Rudolf Steiner describes that the sleep life is different in the first nine years of life and that the real sleep life starts only in puberty.[14] 'Real' sleep is when the astral body is able to reach out during the night into the cosmos, into the spiritual homeland. The etheric body will not do that. During the night, the etheric regenerates our nervous system and sense organs. Sense organs and nervous system are used up and destroyed by conscious daytime activities. In lecture one of Steiner's 1919 course to the teachers of the first Waldorf School, he says, *Children, at the beginning of their earthly existence, cannot yet complete the transition between sleeping and waking in a way appropriate to human beings.*[15]

Children cannot take everything they have experienced physically into the spiritual world, process it there, and then bring it back to the physical plane.

When I first read this, I had to laugh! Surely, in school, children ought to be awake. Why do they need to be taught to sleep? I really couldn't understand what Steiner meant. However, going deeper through my medical studies, I understood better how, during sleep, young children's astral and I-organization are still oriented to develop the physical body. Only the etheric forces are in a process of liberation, but, as yet, not the astral forces at this stage.

If a teacher really knows what they are talking about and feels connected with the truth and wisdom behind and within their words

14 Steiner, R. (1919/1996). *Foundations of human experience*, see footnote 2.
15 Ibid.

when they are talking to their students, then this spiritual quality has a positive effect on children's sleep. It can give the child the same spiritual orientation which the astral body can give later in life. That is, by being able to connect during sleep with the people met during the day and with the beautiful order found in the world of the stars, it replaces, so to speak, the child's inability to go to the essential world of other beings during the night's sleep, which is important for giving the etheric additional impulses for regeneration of its neurosensory system and the night learning. In the time before the liberation of the child's astral body, the teacher can, via the classroom subjects being taught, truthfully and honestly, prepare students for a more health-giving sleep. During the day the children develop an inner, almost unconscious feeling: 'What I learn here is essential and is grounded in both the physical and in the spiritual world.' Then, the sleep of those children will be much healthier.

For me, as a doctor, knowing this, it becomes more and more touching when I read almost every month new studies and research documents about the growing sleeping disorders of children.[16] It is not only increased noise and that everything is faster paced nowadays, but these disorders are also strongly associated with the effect of the Media. The media are 'sleep killers,' not only because they keep children awake longer, but even if children do have enough hours to sleep but they have watched screens for too many hours during the day, then they are not inwardly nourished nor prepared for sleep. Their sleep will then be superficial, neither nourishing nor really health-giving. What we learn through anthroposophy is not just 'nice to have' or 'just a bit relevant.' It is essential that Teacher Faculties in Waldorf schools really study Steiner, even though it is not

16 See research articles supporting screen-free early childhood centers at www. eliant.eu; R. Brinton & M. Glöckler (Eds.). (2019). *Growing up healthy in a world of digital media: A guide for parents and caregivers of children and adolescents* (A. Klee, Trans.). Stroud, UK: InterActions.

so easy to do so. I am convinced that it is increasingly necessary that we really understand about human development, not only from the physical point of view, but also spiritually. We need to understand why so many new problems are appearing.

We are called to understand our conditions, and how human beings can develop healthily. On one side it is essential for us to study child development, and on the other, it is also essential to study the conditions for human beings' healthy development for adult learning. I would like to recommend Rudolf Steiner's book, *Knowledge of the Higher Worlds.*[17] In chapter 5, titled "Requirements (Conditions) for the Inner Path," Rudolf Steiner describes seven conditions for healthy human development: The first requirement is that we turn our attention to the improvement of our physical and mental or spiritual health. Our health does not in the first place depend on us. Yet we can make an effort to improve it. Sound understanding—healthy cognition—occurs only in a healthy human being. Esoteric schooling does not exclude unhealthy people, but demands that they have the will to lead a healthy life. Such health depends upon achieving the greatest possible independence and autonomy.

Reading these conditions, you realize that all learning has conditions (even driving a car has its rules and conditions). When I want to become a truth-oriented human being, I need to keep conditions. I am always the result of the conditions I live in, and that goes for everything in life, even for the humanization process. When I think of the youngsters of today, they need more adults who are adult learners, learning how to develop their humanity, and truth is the fundament of everything which has the name human. I hope you will enjoy reading this chapter of *Knowledge of Higher Worlds* anew, even

---

17 Steiner, R. (1904/1994). *How to know higher worlds* (C. Bamford, trans.) [GA 10]. Great Barrington, MA: Anthroposophic Press. Earlier translated as *Knowledge of higher worlds.*

though most of you will know it well. It is an eye opener to develop learning tools, more truthfulness in life and in the way you handle yourself. I close my attempt to contribute something to the concept of truth in education, self-education (and a little bit about promoting health), with the following verse, which Rudolf Steiner gave to Dr Eugene Kolisko, the first school doctor at the Stuttgart Waldorf School. It was for teachers and doctors to meditate together and learn to support one and other in their daily work to help children and young people humanize and to create a better world. This verse has become the 'Kolisko Conferences' Manifesto, because Dr Kolisko was one of the doctors who received this verse from Steiner, and he was the first who tried it so as to support the teachers in their daily work:

Once, in olden times
There lived in the souls of the Initiates
Powerfully the thought,
That by nature, every person is ill.
And education was seen
as the healing process
Which brought to the child
As it matured,
Health for life's fulfilled humanity.

2: BEAUTY

Yesterday we centered upon the question, "What processing of the content of the Waldorf curriculum helps the child develop a sense for truth?" We heard about four steps in that process. Now, we shall consider the question, "How can I help the child of today develop a sense of beauty?" Truth is primarily related to thinking and observation, beauty is related to our feeling life. Let me focus first on this. The Waldorf curriculum gives content and context to teaching, but what is especially important is the way we use it. It depends upon the methodology and processes that we use in teaching as to what feelings are stimulated and engaged and how the sense for beauty can develop.

Perfection in the animal world compared to the striving of the human being

According to the Chinese calendar of years, this year, 2018, is the year of the dog, or earth dog, to be more precise. According to legend, Buddha, as he was preparing for his death, wanted to say farewell to the animals, but when he called out to them, only twelve came to say goodbye. Buddha then blessed each of the twelve and allotted each animal one year. As there were twelve animals, these have become the twelve years of the Chinese calendar.[18]

In western astronomy and astrology, the path that the sun, moon and planets follow in the heavens is called the ecliptic, and the twelve constellations that lie behind this path are called the zodiac (*zo-on* is Greek for "animal"). Many of the western zodiac signs and constellations were seen as mythological animals, but there are exceptions. For example, Aquarius, the water carrier, was named after a human being and Libra after a balance or scales. What they all have in common is that they are archetypal.

---

18 These are the Rat, Ox, Tiger, Rabbit, Dragon, Snake, Horse, Sheep, Monkey, Rooster, Dog and Pig.

Aquarius may be considered as an 'ideal' human being. Not one of us is an 'Aquarius,' but he is an ideal for the human being. In the art of eurythmy,there are gestures given to eurythmy performers for each sign of the zodiac.[19] Aquarius [demonstrated as part of this lecture: both arms stretched out forward, whilst simultaneously moving, one arm upward, the other downward, then rhythmically alternating] is the only zodiac sign in eurythmy which moves, the others are static. Aquarius is in perfect balance, a beautiful being, with all things just right, yet flexible and adaptable. Through rhythm, we have the possibility to adapt, and the better our rhythmic system, the better are our forces for adaptation.

Libra, the balance or scales in our western zodiac, is a most ideal 'machine.' The pharmacist, at least in ancient times, needed such a very fine scale to measure small parts of milligrams of gold and other precious ingredients. Today we have even more precise weighing machines, but Libra signifies the most ideal machine made by human beings as a mechanical, cultural instrument. Thus, our western zodiac includes animals, technology, and the picture of the balanced, ideal human being.

But why so many animals? Surely not only because they are quite close relatives of humans? We have the same vertebrate system as all the vertebrates, but we use it differently from the rat, rabbit, birds, lions, tigers, elephants, snakes, and so on. What is the difference between humans and animals in the use of the skeleton? The difference is that animals are able to make the most perfect use of their whole bony system, so perfect that they can never fail, cannot

19 Steiner, R. (1924/1984). *Eurythmy as visible speech* (V. & J. Compton-Burnett, trans.) [GA 279, lecture 10]. London: Rudolf Steiner Press.
[Steiner, with a group of eurythmists, showed his audience the eurythmy gestures for the twelve constellations/signs. He described Aquarius as the "human striving for balance," the water man or "Etheric man." – Ed.]

feel guilty, and do everything just right for what they are. They are miracles of completeness. No bird can become more bird-like or 'bird-ier,' no dog 'dog-ier,' no cow 'cow-ier,' nor bee 'bee-ier.' It's impossible! They are perfect by nature. The Kolisko verse which I spoke at the end of yesterday's lecture tells us that "by nature every person is ill." This, one cannot say for the animals. By nature, every animal is perfect, perfectly healthy. When they get old, animals either die or become less able and then they are eaten up, or they just lie down and wait to die. It is part of animal nature to be worthy, strong, healthy and perfect. For humans, it is typical that we can be weak and imperfect. We show struggling, striving, suffering, longing, judging and comparing, and, as I mentioned in yesterday's lecture, we can even develop the desire to destroy and become 'dehumanized.' We are the opposite of being perfect.

In many ancient cultures, including ancient Egypt, the highest beings of the spiritual world, gods and goddesses were symbolized by animals, because animals are the most perfect creatures we can find on earth. The Hebrews were instructed specifically not to create a picture or image of God, because, being so imperfect themselves, they should not create a picture of their creator! On the other hand, we read in the first book of Moses, "God created the human being in His own image." That seems to be a contradiction. We therefore find in the book of Genesis not only one, but two creation stories, which can help to solve this problem. In the first story, after each day's creation, we read, "...and God saw it was good." On the sixth day, after creating the vertebrates and the human being, both male and female, God contemplated His creations and we read, "And God saw that it was very good." That is impressive; at least it was for me when I read it the first time. Why are we very good yet being so imperfect? The answer is given in the second creation story in Genesis, chapter two, which is totally different.

In chapter two, it is said that God took a piece of earth, formed the shape of the human being , blew in His breath and it became a living soul. God placed this human being, Adam, in the Garden of Eden. God thought it is not good that this human being was alone, so He took a rib from Adam and formed out of the bones (the middle part of the human being), the female and named her Eve. The female in this story is not made out of earth; she is made out of living substance from the middle part, the bones of the rhythmic system of the man. Therefore Eve felt free and justified to eat the fruit from the forbidden tree, following her feeling and desire. The male, made out of earth, was given clear instructions how to handle his will. Man represents thinking and will. This is a difference. Eve represents more the middle part of the human being, led by feelings, with breathing, a sense for balance and the 'middle.' Here is beauty 'at home'; she finds the tree beautiful and enjoyable. When we read these mythological pictures of creation, we sense that we humans are definitely different in that we can sense what is right or wrong. Humans as male and female are one-sided; both are incomplete and are not a 'picture of God.' The second creation story continuously leads into the Fall and all the pain of experiencing our incompleteness as well as the joy of conscious love and freedom.

When I was fifteen/sixteen, we studied contemporary history, which included, of course, the Second World War. We learned that at least thirty people tried to kill Hitler, yet none of them was successful. I thought, "If God existed, surely He would have allowed one of these thirty people to kill this monster? Why didn't He do anything? Either God doesn't exist or he has no interest in us." This is typical of how young people can argue when they start to think. We start our own thinking at fifteen or sixteen years. We can use our thinking before that period, during puberty, to argue, but at that earlier stage, our thinking is still dependent, to a high degree, on what we learn to think through others. By fifteen or sixteen years of age, we can feel distanced, quite powerfully, from our spiritual origin and from a concept of God. We want to know why there are so many religions. Which one is the right one, one or none? Is there a need, a space for religion in this world driven by money and material good and values? We are not perfect but we make a start on our own way.

What has all this to do with beauty? The astral body gives us the capacity to feel, to experience polarities, to differentiate, to live in tensions between the negative and the positive, the black and white and all the colors in between, the whole range of sympathies and antipathies. It is giving us the possibility to feel guilt, transformation, the grace of becoming.

The astral body has a different shape in men and women. They are different again in the way they experience themselves as human beings, how they experience others and the world. The astral body is the force of differentiation and therefore it is the power behind wisdom. We are as wise as we can differentiate and relate each point or aspect of life to its whole environment.

Scottus Eriugena[20]: relation of minerals, plants, animals to the human being

Scottus Eriugena, a 9th century Irish monk, had a modern way to teach. He asked his brother monks various questions to make them aware of differentiation in Nature:

First question: *What do human beings have in common with the mineral world?* The answer is their bones, their mineral, physical structures.

---

20 Johannes Scottus Eriugena, d. 877 CE, praised as the "greatest mind of the early western medieval period—or last great mind of Antiquity." *Eriugena* means "Irish-born," where the Scotti were an ancient and extensive tribe. Retrieved from http://www.sophia-project.org/uploads/1/3/9/5/13955288/conway_eriugena.pdf

Second question: *What do human beings have in common with the plant world?*

Eventually, we find the answer is life. But what is this? Rudolf Hauschka, chemist, pharmacist and founder of the anthroposophic pharmaceutical company Wala, asked Steiner, "What is life? How can I engender life in the making of medicines?" Steiner answered, "You need to study rhythms; rhythms are carriers of life, and rhythms can substitute strength."[21] As a school doctor, I had to give the twelfth grade[22] Main Lesson block, Biology of the vertebrates: the human being and the first three years of life. I gave the students an overview of the animal realm, beginning with the single cell; then, quite quickly, we reached the vertebrates. I asked the students, "What is the difference between something which is alive and something which is dead?"

What followed was one of my most touching experiences in teaching. After this question had been raised, the thirty or more students were at first sitting quietly. Then came the first smile and glance, and eventually suggestions began to be made. The more that suggestions were made, the more this class became a large 'ear,' or resonance body for the suggestions as to whether or not students agreed. After ten minutes, they were all together, listening, watching one another and judging each and every suggestion. You could immediately feel and see if the class was in agreement. After thirty minutes, it was astonishing, that so far, there had been no agreement with anything offered. After thirty-five minutes, still no solution. And then one girl made her suggestion, "I think the difference between something which is dead and something which is alive is that something which is alive always needs an environment out of which and for which it is living and a dead thing does not."

---

21 German: 'Rhythmus ersetzt Kraft'
22 Also called Class 12, 17- to 18-year-old students, the final year in a Waldorf school.

There was such a beautiful silence of deepest agreement in that moment. They felt touched by a truth and I experienced what developed this sense of truth: Good questions, time to think, to listen, to try, to go on, to wait. If on one day there is no solution, then carry this question over the night and start the next day under another perspective. This process can develop the feeling for truth, the sense for truth. It is a gift if a teacher has such an experience. Out of these experiences you can form further teaching steps and how you can prepare lessons which might suit the many learning processes of the students. I am sure that many students will keep this experience in their memory, because this moment of understanding was not only an experience of truth, it was a very powerful emotional experience as well, an experience that life is beautiful.

Life is based on rhythm and Steiner's descriptions of Seven Life Processes[23] (Breathing, Warming, Nourishing, Secreting, Maintaining, Growing and Reproducing) are extremely helpful toward understanding life, being just one part of the complex system of laws which we name life, or the etheric. Rudolf Steiner chose the word *etheric* from the Greek language, *ho-aither* or *ether*, which means "blue skylight." Sunlight, upon the beautiful covering of air around the earth, creates this blue light. This light quality is taken in by plants for making their chlorophyll as an energy resource, which then becomes the basis for animal and human nutrition. We can say that all our life comes from the sun, from the 'blue sunlight' or 'sun-ether.' The etheric body is a complex system of rhythms between sun and earth, and these daily rhythms of the sun give us our inner, biological clock. The moon and planets also influence our inner rhythms. Steiner named the etheric system of laws *the etheric organization*. When I speak with mainstream doctors, I find the term *etheric organization* is better understood than the words *etheric body*.

---

23 Steiner, R. (1916/1990). *The riddle of humanity* [GA 170, lectures 7 & 8]. London: Rudolf Steiner Press.

Third question: *What do humans share together with the animals?*

And the answer is the soul, inner and outer movement, and our possibilities to express our inner life; inner, not the outer or biological life. My spirit lives in the soul and I know about my spirit from what I can think, feel and manage myself. What is beyond that horizon I may have, but I am not conscious about it. Because the soul, the astral body, makes us conscious, my 'I' is totally dependent upon that sort of awareness. Therefore the 'I' lives in the soul and it depends on my soul's developmental stage as to how much I know about my 'I,' what concepts I can think, how I feel and how I manage myself. We shall consider the human 'I' in the next lecture, but for today we stay with the astral, which we share with the animals.

But there is a huge exception. At the beginning of this lecture, we thought about the animals of the Chinese cycle of the year and the western zodiac circle. We considered the beauty and perfection of animal species and how, in comparison, humans are not as perfect or specialized as the animals. The human ideal is to be flexible and to strive for balance. We can recognize characteristic virtues and vices attributed to the astrological animal signs within us, but we do not have to follow what the stars have given. We can change our habits and transform ourselves. We can feel ideals and sometimes be more Leo-, Virgo- or Aquarius-like, and so on. We can learn to balance out their virtues and their shadow sides. I can use my typical habits in an unusual way and I can transform, out of my errors, something very good. I can handle my light and shadow sides individually, because I have the whole astral wisdom in my disposition. The animals, although one sided and specialized, are fully expressive of their emotions and feelings and characters. Each animal is beautiful in its completeness and form, and we sense their beauty. We can love good films about animals because we are touched by how they live and behave so appropriately to their forms in which inner and outer are in harmony. That is beauty, when everything is just as it should be. Something appears beautiful if a being can completely reveal itself and the inner experience and the outer expression are in balance. There is a beautiful anecdotal conversation between the Dutch painter, Bernhard von Orly, and the German, Albrecht Dürer. Dürer: "Raphael brought the Madonna's heaven onto earth in his painting." Orly: "But, you, dear Dürer, you bring back the earth to heaven through your perception." He admired the way Dürer was seeing and painting plants and animals in their utmost completeness. Beauty is a balancing of the heavenly and earthly experiences. Therefore the arts in the forms of speech, drama, singing, music, sculpture and painting have such powerful healing aspects and can bring peace and harmony to the feeling life.

We humans have beauty as an ideal. We can strive for beauty. We can learn by experience to judge what is really aesthetic and beautiful. However, if we do not undergo an education which develops our sense for beauty, or, as Rudolf Steiner expresses it, 'our aesthetic sense,' then we can lose the sense for beauty. We have all witnessed instances where sympathy is shown toward the ugly, the destructive or toward humorless sarcasm. Humor is in the aura of beauty. Sarcasm is in the aura of the destructive. Today, we can experience that humanity has not only lost the sense for truth because education is business/career/requirements-oriented rather than truth-oriented. When I look at some of the mainstream, commercially produced booklets intended for first, second and third graders to write or color in, I sense that in many cases, from childhood on, the sense for balance, harmony and beauty is being suppressed, deformed and even erased. If something in the human being is suppressed, the counter forces can grow, and the balance of keeping the middle between the two extremes becomes lost. The counter force of a suppressed sense of beauty is hatred and sympathy for the destructive. Hatred of something which is beautiful is a destructive desire, such as the tragic events of mass shootings (the latest occurring only last week in a high school in Florida). Such events will become more frequent if education remains so 'un-aesthetic.' The counter reaction of a suppressed sense of aesthetic and harmony is aggression, a desire to kill harmony.

Bernd Ruf[24] is in the executive team of Friends of Waldorf Education,[25] which supports emergency relief for disaster relief worldwide (e.g., the 2011 Japanese tsunami, earthquake and nuclear disaster). He founded the Parzival School in Karlsruhe (see www.parzival-zentrum. de/), into which children and students are welcomed who cannot be integrated into public schools, such as those who are most neglected, are drop outs or have criminal and destructive tendencies. Bernd Ruf wanted to create an appropriate environment for them, inspired by Rudolf Steiner's ideas:

...Every education is self-education and we, as teachers and educators, are only part of the environment in which the child can then educate itself... in relationship to its inner destiny.[26]

Self-activity is the mystery of Waldorf education and a Waldorf school architect aims to create spaces so that children can act in an age-appropriate, self-active manner. Ruf sought for the right physical environment for such criminally minded, hate-filled, destructive youngsters which would help them to behave differently than previously. Together with an anthroposophic architect, he designed an archetypal Waldorf school building with good proportions, colors, and aesthetic pictures as he thought the ideal Waldorf school should be. A huge school yard was incorporated into the design for all sorts

---

24 Ruf, B. (2013). *Educating traumatized children, Waldorf education in crisis intervention*. (M.M Saar, trans.) New York: Lindisfarne Books.
25 See www.freunde-waldorf.de/en/
26 Steiner, R. (1923/1988). *The child's changing consciousness as the basis of pedagogical practice* (R. Everett, trans.) [GA306, lecture 6]. Hudson, NY: Anthroposophic Press

of animals (such as llamas), to benefit those children who best learn to communicate, at first, through animals. All in all, they designed a beautiful environment for all the different needs. Ruf was convinced that, because these students were still in development, their hatred against a beautiful environment could not yet be as fixed as could be the case in adults. The sense for beauty can be trained, because the beautiful gives us the impression, 'do not touch me.' When we see something very beautiful, we become sensitive, we want to protect the beautiful. That was Ruf's concept.

Money was needed, and the City of Karlsruhe offered a certain amount, as they had a high interest in the establishment of such a school, but to complete the financing, a further million euros more was needed to come from other sponsors. Ruf's ideas were presented to a charitable foundation. However, when they saw the classic, anthroposophic Waldorf design of the architecture, they asked for something more modern and progressive. Their offer was: Finance and a new design, or no money and then you can go with your classic Waldorf design. Ruf explained why these students needed to have the design as proposed: Proportions of architecture are something that students see all the time they are in school; the way the walls are painted, the way the classroom is organized, what clothes the teachers wear, the way the blackboard is oriented—all these are daily influences on the students' sense of the aesthetic.

Youngsters, with destructive emotions who have not developed their sense for beauty and who hate the harmonious, are however, still in development. Ruf was convinced that if such youngsters were to sit in a classroom in which they permanently saw the beautiful, the harmonious in all details (and teachers would be well trained in this regard), then they could recapitulate, to a certain extent, what they had missed in their earlier years. When a student did do something destructive, like spraypaint or destroy things, teachers, parents and some students would come overnight to make the destruction disappear, and the next morning, it would be as though nothing had happened. This would teach the students that no one was angry and that they could not provoke, it would make no sense. If this were experienced two or three times, they would stop. When Ruf explained such things to the city authorities, as to why he would not change the classic design of the architecture in order to receive the million euros from the charity, the city of Karlsruhe said, "Herr Ruf, this is convincing, we want you to do it exactly how you want it and we shall give you the extra million." This story is also an example of courage. Money is wonderful but only if handled freely, and we are not bought and made dependent upon it.

Astral organization development, from birth to 7 years

In early childhood, during the incarnating of the astral body, the only way it can excarnate is via the senses, when it is together with the etheric. The senses are developing in the first seven or eight years of life through the way we take charge of them and by how we use them. The etheric makes the shapes and the astral senses what is seen. To learn differentiated feelings through every little differentiated sense experience, the child is allowed to sense. We have a word in German (*Empfindung*) for this sensing or sensitivity, which has no real equivalent in English. It is not an emotion but is an extremely pure, very tender, gentle feeling or impression, a sensing of what you see. If it's a beautiful flower, red, green, your fine-feeling reaction you are sensing is different, depending on what you look at and also on the time you give yourself to resonate with what you see.

The astral and the etheric have a very close connection. The astral makes conscious that which lives in the etheric. Therefore those sensations which come to mind and can make us conscious, inspired and provoked by what we see and hear and touch and so on, these are the objective educators of our feeling life. If you feel the beauty of a rose, you have an objective feeling and that is a sensation. It is not your emotion. But your astral body can then feel drawn to this sensation and then there is a transition between these pure sensations which is objective. You feel the other through a basis of empathy, that you are with the other, and not how you are with your projection into the other. You really feel the other. But then you can also make this pure objective feeling more and more your own emotion, so there is a transition depending upon how you deal with your sense expressions.

So, in the first seven years, the astral body has this beautiful education through the sense experiences during the time in which the aesthetic sense is grounded. Therefore for the first seven years of life, Rudolf Steiner says, "The world must be good."[27] Children need to see good things, good deeds, so that they can develop the feeling for what is good, for what is beautiful, for what is true, because all these three help to make the world appear really good.

From yesterday's lecture, we saw that the good cannot be isolated from beauty and truth, nor beauty from the good and true; likewise nor truth from beauty and goodness. The thinking aspect of observation leads to a sense for the truth; the feeling aspect of observation leads the child to a sense of beauty, of the aesthetic; and when they do and observe actions, they can develop a sense for the good.

Astral organization development in the second seven years– from 7 to 14

In the second period between seven and fourteen, the astral forces liberate from their activity within the physical constitution and develop the whole range of 'out of body' emotional life. But what

---

27 Steiner, R. (1907/1996). "The education of the child in the light of spiritual science," in *The education of the child and early lectures on education* (pp. 1–39). Hudson, NY: Anthroposophic Press.

is an emotion? We think about hormones, neurotransmitters, the rhythmic system, because if we react emotionally, we change the way of breathing etc. From a spiritual point of view emotions and feelings are the 'out of body' or body-free astral activity accompanied by physiological processes, which are not the origins of but they are the result of the astral activity.

Astral development in the third seven year period: 14–21 years

In the third seven years, fourteen to twenty-one, the astral body has a next step in its development. This step, which occurs once puberty commences, is the most delicate and needs to be prepared in our Waldorf curriculum from the very beginning. Our task is to help the astral body of youngsters to become more and more independent from the desires of the body and to learn to adapt to the realm of thinking. Steiner in his lectures to the teachers of the first Waldorf School says:

In education, we are quite often concerned with the question of separating feeling from willing. When freed from willing, feeling then connects itself with thinking cognition and is concerned with it in later life. We properly prepare children for later life only when we enable them to successfully separate feeling from willing. Later, as men or women, they can connect their free feeling with thinking cognition and, thus, fully meet life.[28]

When you feel what you think, then your astral body reveals its utmost greatest power of differentiation, because nothing is as complicated as our thinking. In our will, life is simple; we can only do one thing after the other. As you write, you make one letter after the other, if you don't do this, then you will not be able to read it afterward! So, our will is simple, one step after the other. But our thinking is multi-

---

28 Steiner, R. (1919/1996). *The foundations of human experience* (R.F. Lathe, trans.) [GA 293, lecture 7, p. 123]. Great Barrington, MA: Anthroposophic Press.

tasking; you have the overview and you have the detail. The astral body is the body of differentiation, and therefore the more we allow it to differentiate, the better it is educated. This is the task in high school.

To conclude Scottus's third question, "What do human beings have in common with the animals?" the answer is, the soul. The soul has a vastly differentiated wisdom which has its most beautiful counterpart in nature in the animal realm, because they are so perfect in performing their lives and showing their emotions.

Fourth question: *What have the humans in common with the angels?*

The answer is: Thinking. Every thought is a message. You cannot smell or touch thinking. You cannot see it, it's a spiritual message, and you can only think it. And what does *angel* mean? *Angelus* is a Greek word meaning "messenger." *Arch-angelus* means "messenger of the origin," these are the Archangels. They know the origin of humans. The Archai, time spirits, go back to the origin of the world, not only of the humans. They are all messengers. But the angels are the messengers closest to us, so we have thinking in common with the angels. Thomas Aquinas was named Pater Angelicus, 'Angel Father,' because people felt he communicated already in pure, true thinking with the angels. After these four questions about what humans have in common with mineral, plant, animal and angel, Scottus asks:

Fifth question: *What has the human being for his own self?*

What is the task of the human being to which only the human being can contribute? No realm of nature will give it to him, no angel realm will give it to him, and he has to do it totally alone out of his own forces. The answer: Practice of independent judgment; good, fair judgment, when you are able to put minor details appropriately into context. Balanced, good judgment comes when you know the meaning of something in its context or in mind. Those who are connected can then feel, "Yes that is right." For example, the student in Grade 12 who answered the question, "What is the difference between something living and something dead?" had made a judgment about life and death. Her classmates knew she was right and that it was a good judgment. She had placed her words appropriately and in the context of understanding, and that is a fair judgment. To be able to judge what is true and beautiful and what is good, that is our humanity. The highest ideal of Waldorf education is to educate to the truly human, to this ability for a fair judgment.

What processing of the content of the Waldorf curriculum helps the child to develop a sense of beauty? The first step toward a sense of beauty is an extremely sensitive care for what the children have to see in the school. How beautiful, how balanced, how well judged, how is everything so in place that the senses are not harmed?

Secondly, of course, we offer parent education and adult learning. Many Waldorf schools have that, but not all parents are able to, or do attend. Concentrate on the hours you have with the children and do your very best for them, but also offer to the parents as much as possible about how they can protect and nurture their children at home.

Can we really understand how the sense of beauty needs to be nourished through the senses? We need to expose the etheric body repeatedly to beautiful sense impressions in order to develop the aesthetic sense, which is this combination of the etheric and the astral. Therefore in our curriculum we have so much activity in kindergarten and the first school years where singing and playing music is done alongside painting and free play. Later we can practice speech exercises, communication exercises, little plays and performances and dramas, in which children can learn to experience all these aesthetic activities. In our artistic lessons on color, we can ask, "Which is more beautiful? Is it when the blue is within and the yellow surrounds it, or is it the other way round?" These manifold aesthetic questions help.

The teacher learns to draw in front of the class so that the children can imitate a person struggling with the beautiful. It can be awkward or discouraging during a lesson if the teacher were to open the blackboard to reveal to the children only the 'perfect' end result of their strivings. It is better not to show such a ready-made picture, but to draw in front of the children. The drawing can be simpler, or use your holidays to take a painting course, to learn what you want your children to learn. If you think the children will learn to do something that you are not able to, or if you are not willing to learn, then they cannot copy you and will dislike your teaching. And yet they need to copy you.

Using our senses, we are lifelong imitators. We copy what we see, we sense what we see, and therefore teachers need to be models when we want to develop the sense for beauty. We need really to be models in all that we do and strive to be better, a little bit at a time. As a striving human being, to get the best possible from your children, you might even say in your class, "Who can make this freehand circle more round than I was able to? I am not so skilled maybe as some of you." Be honest, and then the sense for the beautiful can develop. It is a process. It is not a miracle, it falls not from heaven. It needs years to develop.

3: GOODNESS

To wonder at Beauty, stand guard over Truth,
Look up to the Noble, resolve on the Good:
This leads us truly, to purpose in living,
To right in our doing, to peace in our feeling,
To light in our thinking,
And teaches us trust, in the workings of God,
In all that there is,
In the widths of the world,
In the depths of the soul.

— Rudolf Steiner

Good morning dear friends,

This beautiful verse, "At the Ringing of Bells," with which we have begun our lectures each morning, is a special verse. It is beautiful, true and really good. It was given by Rudolf Steiner to a boy of about eight years old. The boy was oppositional, teachers couldn't handle him; he was a so-called difficult child, whose parents thought he would never become a 'normal' human being. His parents, as anthroposophists, went to Dr Steiner for advice. Steiner then spoke with this lad, and gave this verse to him. Because this verse has the curious title rather than, perhaps, a title mentioning Truth, Beauty and Goodness, this is what I think Steiner might have said to this boy:

"I know you will become a perfect boy. I know this already, but other people do not see this yet; therefore you get into trouble and also with the other children. So, whenever you hear the bells ringing, think about this verse, which has within it the secret of how to become the good person that you are. Each time you hear the bells ringing and remember that you have this good companion, then the more you will show that you are on your way toward becoming the very good person we know already that you are, even though, as yet, not everyone can see it properly.`

When we first look at this verse, it appears very idealistic. Normal life is not like that. But by speaking and hearing it, each time, we can begin to feel the truth, peace, honesty and love within it. We feel the ideal of how to become a true human being. We all know that the way to realize these ideals is a lifelong struggle and journey. Therefore, I am so happy that we can hear this verse each morning, because it shows the whole meaning of this conference. We are here in service of children, who all have to learn, but we are also here in the service of our own higher being. We all struggle with how to focus and concentrate our best forces toward that higher goal, to take another step, and to refresh our awareness of what is and what is not essential.

This verse leads into the most complex question, that is, the question about Goodness. Firstly however, I wish to share some 'resonances' from our previous days' themes of Truth and Beauty:

Truth is an easily accessible ideal. We have all experienced what is true, and we know how poisoning untruthfulness is. We all, more or less, at least in our private life, have a high appreciation for honesty between people. So, truth is very close to us.

Beauty, however, is already a bit further removed, as it depends a lot upon our own aesthetic education. What is the process which really educates us to see real beauty? Beauty does not mean that something is perfect. Beauty means that all the factors, in one particular moment, are in balance. For example, a germinating plant already has its own beauty at that stage of development; next, when the sprout comes up, it is again in another state of beauty. For each stage of becoming, we see that each stage has its own beauty because it is in a process, in a balanced interaction with its environment. We can train our observation so as to see from where each stage comes, to where it might go next, and then we can contemplate this beautiful balanced-out moment in between.

I mentioned yesterday, the importance of the child's seeing the **process** of how a picture or a form emerges, because that is part of the beautiful, and the process which leads to the final balanced momentum. When Rudolf Steiner held lectures, he often drew at the blackboard while he was speaking. This was also the case when he gave courses for the teachers. He created sketches and drawings directly in front of his audience. This is in stark contrast to today's popular custom of using power point presentations or of distributing complete, finished hand outs to the audience. During the first year of school, this principle of 'allowing pictures to grow before the eyes of the children' is especially important. Through such a process, the natural imitative ability of the children is addressed. At the same time, the possibility is given for the children to follow the creative or 'becoming' processes (German: *Werdeprozesse)*. The teacher acts as a welcome authority and the whole process builds toward a worthy goal from beginning to end. Van James, in his book, *Drawing with Hand, Head and Heart*,[29] quotes Rudolf Steiner, who said, as he was drawing:

I have made drawings before your eyes that arose wholly out of each moment. You could see what I meant by every stroke. You could think along with me without any mediation. This is another thing to be included in teaching children today. As much as possible ,avoid finished drawings and allow the children to see the drawing proceeding from the moment. Allow them to see each stroke as it is born. In this way the child becomes inwardly involved in the work and we encourage them to become inwardly active. What matters is to lead the children into independence. The more we make children inwardly active, the more we support their independence.[30]

29 James, V. (2012) *Drawing with hand, head and heart: A natural approach to learning the art of drawing*. Great Barrington, MA: Lindisfarne Books.
30 Steiner, R. (1997). *Knowledge of higher worlds: Rudolf Steiner's blackboard drawings* (pp. 22–23). Berkeley, CA: University of California, Berkeley Art Museum and Pacific Film Archive.

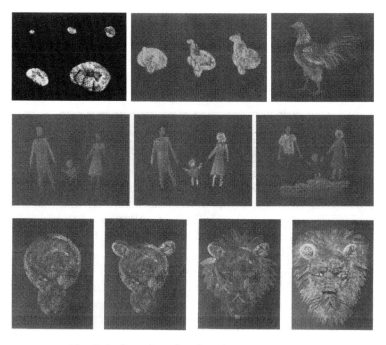

Fig. 3.1 Growing the drawing – Van James

Years 0 to 7

During the first seven years, children become both physically and inwardly active in their body. We create an environment in which children can move freely. They do not need an adult to tell them where to go or where to stop. For example, we try not to cut or break children's crawling intentions. So, where does a child stop? It stops when there is a natural barrier and the child experiences resistance. The world has limits, so the child finds a limitation and is stopped. On meeting physical boundaries, the child can look for another orientation and create a plan B as to what to do next; all that is a physical experience, programmed by the brain. Later on in life we can make mental experiences about limitation, benchmarks, and conditions and so on. Without ever really having these physical experiences, the concept of limitations would not be based on reality. It would be relative. The development of physical freedom, in which we move out of a free intention and have an environment which educates our intentionality, is good in the most natural given way. Limits are good if they are on the right place. In contrast, if an adult is commanding or shouting, "Don't touch that! Come off! That's not good. You are bad, be nice!," that is the worst when the child's intention is broken at this early stage, and a few years later we hear complaints that the adolescent lacks motivation! Physicians and psychologists are then asked to try to compensate, which saddens me. To summarize, during the first seven years we aim to create conditions for free play, movement, fantasy and free inner activity.

Years 7–14

During the so-called 'time of authority' (loving authority), between seven and fourteen years, this inner free activity as described leads the child to be able to follow what the adult is doing and learn to follow instructions freely. To be surrounded by Beauty will develop the child's sense for beauty for example, by the way the teacher is acting, processing, having the whole classroom in order and in balance. Beauty is in the balanced moment. The child cannot create such meaningful interactions by themselves, but they can learn through experiencing an adult interacting in this way. Authority does not mean, "I am the big boss and there are the children who have to follow me." That would be authoritarian. But authority means that the children experience an author, an 'auto,' or adult self, which allows them to find the conditions for becoming autonomous in their own soul.

Authority in the best sense of the word means that the child experiences an adult who is striving , struggling and dares to expose him or herself as an 'I am.' A true authority is honest in his attempts and can be a real friend, partner and guide. Partners, in the sense that the child is a becoming, developing being, but so is the teacher, although older, and some steps further. That is what makes them partners. Life becomes beautiful if we feel as brothers and sisters in becoming and the one who is two steps in front of the other can show the other how to do it. Not, 'copy me,' but instead, 'see what you think is correct, and try out of your own inner, soul activity to do the same, but in your own way.'

In 2010, when I was last here in Hawai'i, I may have mentioned my eye opener for this mystery of education, for beauty. It is related to what Steiner means by characterizing, instead of defining. The whole of teaching must be artistic between 7 and 14 years. Artistic education means that authority comes about through characterizing, through my showing the children that I am striving and doing my best. This artistry begins already in the first lesson in the first grade when the teacher, out of authority, brings awareness of the verticality and the curve to the children.

Fig.3.2 Straight line and curve

Through the will for change, action and re-forming, the teacher shows that they know what is straight and what is curvy in the world. However, when the children draw these lines in their booklets, their attempts can be very different. The teacher's task is then to characterize each child's attempt, without judging them as right or wrong, ugly or good or beautiful. To judge them would be to define them. Rather, the aim is to see where each child is in their striving to find verticality and the curve. Where is this child in his striving to be able to make their hand follow a thought? We can traumatize children through our judgments and definitions, for example, by promoting those children who make the best booklet or score best on a test, or by always choosing the same children to receive their booklets back first or get special praise. Sometimes they even get a star on the blackboard, which means that those children who already know they are not the best are reminded about being last again and again. These children can leave school thinking, "I am not good in comparison with the others, and I was always last." Instead, such children need to experience, "I am as good as I can be, I did my best and someone could see it. I am not alone, my self-acknowledgment is not alone, and there are also others who see my striving. I am not a dropout. No, I am a drop-in!"

My personal wakeup experience for this mystery was my observation of a Class One teacher, in his introduction to the letters. He began by telling an interesting and beautiful story about the letter 'T.' Toward the end of the story, with its descriptions of battles and all sorts of interesting things, the heroes of the story sat at a large wooden table. Out of his drawing of the table, the letter 'T' was distilled. Then it was the children's turn, to first draw the 'T' shape in the air, and then they were allowed to walk it so as to make it a complete body experience. Next the children sounded it out, 't, t, t,' searching for words with the 't' sound at the beginning, end or in the middle of words, so it became an acoustic experience. Finally, he asked, "Who is now willing to come to the blackboard and try to draw the T?" A boy who was sitting quite close to me at the back of the class immediately raised his hand. He went forward, and half way to the blackboard, I saw already how his courage was waning and his last steps were very slow. He approached the blackboard, drew, right in the corner, his very small version of T, and rushed back to his seat.

Here and there, a little laughter started to arise in the class and I thought; "Now this child will get his first school trauma and will not raise his hand so quickly in future and he will be a little bit damaged." My school doctor's heart was beating. How will the teacher manage this situation so that it remains a beautiful experience? The teacher was a young Waldorf teacher, who had studied and this was his first

Fig. 3.3 Child's version of capital T

class. At first, he said nothing. He didn't laugh; he just looked at the boy's drawing, and then looked at the boy, saw the lad's red face and the laughter stopped. The children looked at the teacher. "Why is he looking in this way? Why he is not laughing or judging?" Then the teacher said, "Children, that is an interesting table. I wonder, who of you has already seen such a table as our boy has presented to us?" There was deep silence in the classroom and the first acknowledging looks went to this boy, as he had made something special and the teacher was reflecting what it was. One girl raised her hand and said, "I know, in my father's office, are such tables, but something is missing." The teacher invited her to come to the blackboard and asked, "What office has your father got?" She replied, "My father is an architect and there is this piece missing, so that pens cannot roll down."

Fig 3.4 Architect's table with a ledge

The girl was praised that she had made the missing link to make this table beautiful. The boy was totally rehabilitated. He had made an architect's table! The teacher could now say, "Next question, who would like to draw the table we had in our story, or another one, like our friend's?"

I had just witnessed an artistic faculty, playfulness and a beautiful process that characterized the letter T. It had been described from different sides, brought into movement and process again. What was in danger to get 'stuck' and end up in unfair judgment was instead led by an authority who knew that the artistic faculty is the faculty of 'becoming.' It is the mobility of our soul in every moment to contribute to the beauty of life with a lot of different tools, the ability to develop such flexibility so that we become aware of what is missing, and that we have an archetype of what is a whole, in harmony. We realize this is something we can approach but that only really great artists can show the completeness.

I hope you can see that this concept of beauty cannot be separated from truth and goodness. Beauty belongs to the middle part of the human being. If the environment is good for a young child, then the child's physical intentionality can act out freely. Once this intentionality becomes active in the soul, children will sit still during controlled movements such as reading and painting. We can be physically still for fifty minutes or so. Our body's free soul forces can then develop and become activated. The intentionality of the 'I' learns to direct those soul forces which are already more or less free. The full 'I am' capacity is still within the body of the child and not yet free.

Years 14–21

The I-organization becomes free only after puberty; therefore the 'I' of the adult replaces the not yet born 'I' forces of the child. The child's intention has already been trained physically through early childhood and is now on the way to be trained in the emotional faculties, which become fully free only when we reach eighteen or nineteen years of age. It is a gradually liberating process which it is very important to realize.

Question: concerning Rudolf Steiner's lecture on *Truth, Beauty and Goodness*[31]

0–7	– Goodness
7–14	– Beauty
14–21	–Truth

In each of the stages of development, you can prepare for all three qualities, but the domain of goodness belongs especially from 0–7, beauty from 7–14, and truth from 14–21.

Nietzsche: *What you do out of love is always beyond good and evil.*

Karl Georg Niebergall:[32] *The true and the beautiful, we need to love, but the good, we need to train.*

Plato's concept of the good embraced also the power of creation, in that the good belongs totally to the Creator, who created the so-called good and the so-called evil. Both embraced the true good which is the content of our whole creation. Aristotle and the following philosophers did not embrace this concept of the Good. They began with good and evil in our daily life and then tried to define what is good. Endless philosophical strivings or 'ethics' were based on that argument. Ethics deal with only the good deed (the word *ethic* or *ethos*, in Greek, means "good deed").

---

31 Steiner, R. (1923/1986). *Truth, beauty and goodness* [GA 220]. Spring Valley, NY: St. George Publications.
Editor's note: Dr Glöckler's response also included comments on the effects of the media, information technology, and the work of ELIANT.
32 Prof Dr Karl Georg Niebergall: Retrieved April; 29, 2018, from https://www.philosophie.hu-berlin.de/en/personen-en/mitarbeiter/1684288

The concept of good in the beginning of philosophy with Plato was that it is the creation as such and that is an attribute of God, not of the human being. Therefore, no human being can be 'good.' These concepts we also find in the Gospels. In the Gospel of St. Luke, a certain ruler asks Jesus, "Good Master, how can I obtain eternal life?" Jesus replies, "Why do you name me good, as good belongs alone to our Father in heaven." (Luke 18:18 King James' Version)[33] Christ does not identify with the attribute good, yet He does identify with truth, saying, "Ye shall know truth and truth shall set you free." (John 4:32 King James' Version) That means if He is the truth, we can find the way to freedom through Christ by understanding truth, by developing our own autonomy.

Christ cannot be the creator of our autonomy; this would be a contradiction in itself. We have to do it by our selves, but He can show us how to find our way for truth and to learn to go alone, to develop our 'I am.' That is His mission, and then we will become free. This journey is good, although very painful, and we have to struggle with evil on that pathway.

We find this concept of the good in Steiner's lectures[34] in which he says that in the first seven years of life, we need to create an environment which is good; that is, an environment primarily that holds an attitude of 'reverence for God.' Teachers, caregivers, parents can feel as representatives of God, the master of evolution. Adults might ask, "Who is this child before us, which shows such great trust as to choose us as his door into this physical world? How can we create the environment so that this child can both find himself

33 See also John 1:17: "The law was given by Moses, but grace and truth came by Jesus Christ."
34 Steiner, R. (1907/1996). "The education of the child in the light of spiritual science." In The education of the child and early lectures on education (pp. 1–39). Hudson, NY: Anthroposophic Press.

and also experience that creation is also there to help us, as adults, to help our own development?" We want the child to feel justified, welcomed, seen and accepted in his environment; not possessed, manipulated or feeling as an object, but to feel as a being of his own.

The good is an attitude we can develop only when we connect with our higher self. As long as we think that good is the opposite of evil, we have not understood what might be the good. We can understand the good only through the doorway of initiation. We can access beauty and truth before we cross the threshold, from this side of the visible world. However, to find Goodness, we need to cross the threshold in order to find it. To find what might be the good in a certain situation, we need to be free from our own wishes and needs. Only then can we be fully connected with the needs of others and develop the right intuition as to what that might be. We must be able to cross the threshold between us and the other. Therefore the Kolisko verse, given by Steiner, has in its center the concept of initiation. Working toward an understanding the threshold between the world of the senses and the spiritual world is crucial within the cooperation of doctors and teachers in service of the new generations. I shall close with this verse, to lead us into the summarizing lecture tomorrow:

Once, in olden times, there lived in the souls of the Initiates
powerfully the thought that by nature every person is ill
and education was seen as the healing process,
which brought to the child as it matured,
health, for life's fulfilled humanity.

— Rudolf Steiner

Fig. 3.5 Growing the drawing – refer James, V. footnote 29

"Drawing a plant should start with a seed and progress through the stages of its unfolding in an organic, natural manner. In this way the drawing is true to the nature of the plant, the ecology of nature."

4: The 'I AM' in relation to Truth, Beauty and Goodness

Dear friends,

I would like to address any questions you have now, so that we can integrate them into this morning's contribution.

Question—*Please relate Steiner's perspectives of truth, beauty and goodness to economics and technology.*

These three qualities are the most human we have, and they can appear as guiding stars in any field of life. It is true that all humanists since Plato regarded these three concepts or ideals as being so elevated that human beings can never realize them here and now. They have to strive throughout their whole life for them. Truth, Beauty and Goodness are the heavenly bread, the mana, so to speak, out of which we can nourish our humanity at any time, place, within any profession. They are our divine human nature, which we can achieve only through many lifetimes and many new attempts. To give a short answer: If economics and technology are serving life, are developed out of the perception of the concrete needs humans have all over the world, then these three stars are shining brightly. If both are serving egocentric win/maximization of desires, beyond the needs of man and nature, then the clouds of materialistic thinking are covering the stars. But let me explain it in a broader context.

Rudolf Steiner connects truth, beauty and goodness with our super-sensible bodies. The physical body integrates all the laws which work in solid matter, including the technological world, as it works with solid matter and physical laws. Technology projects the faculties of our physical body. Firstly, machines replaced our muscle skills, next our feeling skills through the technological advances in measuring instruments (technologies/techniques), and finally, in our time, information/communication technology offers a projection of the brain activity. We are happy when machines do our work and serve us. But we suffer enormously if technology dominates us or, through weapons technologies, is destroying us. We can see immediately that 'goodness' is the main challenge as to how to use technologies. Rudolf Steiner said, in this context, that the technological development must be accompanied by an education leading to high moral faculties. Ray Kurzweil, futurist and director of engineering at Google, founded Project 2045.[35] This is a trans-humanistic project, to enable human individual intelligence to be transported into a computer placed in a robot carrying our shape. Through this transformation from the biologically based intelligence to a technologically based one, humans can survive their consciousness and 'survive' eternally in an Avatar. This project aims to be ready by 2045. In my view, the trans-humanists are highly motivated to adapt toddlers to the digital world, so that they learn to live together with their electronic devices from the beginning and learn that this is the source of 'true life.' This is the spirituality behind this movement, a spirituality of only the physical. I perceive a connection between the trans-humanists' aims with Rudolf Steiner's descriptions of a spiritual being, Ahriman,[36] who wishes to transform the Earth into a new Saturn.[37] Human beings would be transformed into intelligent machines, with a new, eternal life on earth, beyond pain or death. Materialists view intelligence only as physical intelligence. All this is not science fiction: it is really thought by those who want to design another way to live on earth than the truly human one. There would be consciousness, but without feeling, pain, death and all other 'unnecessary' ingredients.

---

35 Kurzweil, R. (2005). *The singularity is near: When humans transcend biology.* New York: Viking. See also: Kurzweil, R. (2000). *The age of intelligent machines.* Cambridge, MA: MIT Press.

36 Steiner, R. (1919/1976) *Lucifer and Ahriman* [GA 193]. Vancouver, Canada: Steiner Book Centre, Inc.

37 Steiner, R. (1910/1997). *An outline of esoteric science* (C.E. Creeger, trans.) [GA 13]. Hudson, NY: Anthroposophic Press.

In our age of Information technology, humanity will, at least for a time, separate into two. Those with a more spiritually orientated point of view will see that our true goal is to transform and spiritualize matter, so as to enter the spiritual world with the fruits of individualization on earth. Our incarnation on earth gives us the chance to individualize, to find ourselves as individuals. That is the gift of the physical body. We 'embody' our unique individual bodies in order to learn that we are individual. We can then take our developed individual human consciousness back into the spiritual world, due to our etheric, astral and I-organization. Materialists on the other hand, will use technology for their purposes. Trans-humanization aims to have eternal life with an individual consciousness, but as a machine. In October 2011, as part of the project, Immortality 2045, the Russian billionaire, Dmitry Istkov, in close cooperation with other trans-humanist's worldwide, spoke of the need for a new, or 'neo-humanity,' with a new ethic and paradigm of what it is to be human.[38] He wanted to re-define the whole of human existence and take it to a trans-humanistic vision, by finding the rules and guidelines of how this should be done. Such intentions as these make me very sensitive about the effects of information technology. We are so 'smart' with our technology, without really knowing what lies behind it. We need to work, not with fear, but with the realization that its limits are in the physical.

What is it the service technology can give me for my human life? At what point do inhuman, or 'de-humanization' tendencies begin? That is the question: How do I find the good? Yesterday, I mentioned the research published on our website, www.eliant.com[39] which, for example, shows which ages of childhood are in most danger

38 Istkov, D. (2012, November 16). *The path to neo-humanity as the foundation of the ideology of the "Evolution 2045" party.* Retrieved July 17, 2018, from http://2045.com/articles/30869.html
39 European Alliance of Initiatives for Applied Anthroposophy. See footnote 4.

from technology, also what are the most prominent side effects of computer addiction. Harmful effects include a lack in the areas of: empathy, concentration, thinking and literacy. The physical body loses its limits and obesity is increasing because children do not move, losing their desire to be active. These problems relate to our theme of what is good and what is beautiful. The trans- or neo-humanists say that pain, illness and death, should not be there. But the mission of death is spiritual awakening and the mission of pain is for us to wake up to something essential that we have not yet thought about before. Pain helps us overcome ego-centrism. Steiner speaks of there being as much pain in the world as there is ego-centrism.[40] If we suffer pain, we can feel that we are out of balance. Egocentrism is in humanity, although it does not have to be our own egocentricity. Such thoughts are spiritual points of view for the same phenomena that the trans-humanists are facing. We are free to make our decisions. Counter pictures of humanity from both sides—the Spiritual and the materialistic—can help us to come to our free choice of what sort of being we want to become.

When I was a student in my first year of study, I had a good friend from my philosophy class and we discussed the meaning of freedom. I was complaining of this and of that and then suddenly he said something very true. "Michaela, you know, freedom is not nice. It is not nice. It really is freedom, so don't complain that bad things are happening." That is freedom. It is a zero point. Out of nothing, we have to make our decisions. If not, we depend either upon good spirits or upon evil inspirations, but then we would not be doing it out of our own self. The ideals of Truth, Beauty and Goodness are like guiding stars. I prepared a verse by Rudolf Steiner for today, which I shall give at the conclusion of this lecture.

---

40 Steiner, R. (1910/1995). *Manifestations of karma* (H. Herman-Davey, trans.) [GA 120, lecture 7]. London: Rudolf Steiner Press.

Question—*Could you please speak about the "Kolisko Verse" and its meaning?*

> *Once, in olden times, there lived in the souls of the Initiates,*
> *powerfully the thought, that by nature, every person is ill*
> *and education was seen as the healing process,*
> *which brought to the child as it matured,*
> *health, for life's fulfilled humanity.*

– Rudolf Steiner

Line 1: *Initiates*—Initiation, in this verse, has to do with the 'zero point,' which I mentioned before. *Initiation* is a Latin word, meaning 'to start.' To 'initiate' something means to give the impulse or start something. An initiation moment is a starting moment. Out of what do you start; through a push from somewhere else, out of convention, duty or desire? What is your intention? Or do you start out of nothing, out of your own pure will, your 'I am me' directed intention?

Line 2: *By nature, every person is ill.* By nature, human beings are incomplete. Health is completeness. If we are healthy, nothing is missing, but by nature, we are not complete. Only animals and plants are complete by nature; therefore they are healthy by nature.

When animals live together with humans, and become dependent upon us, they can also succumb to our disorders. The animal changes. Humans have a transformative effect, not only in matter but also upon animals and plants. Some people have a flourishing garden and others not. Humans are the masters of evolution because they are allowed to direct their evolution themselves. But they pay for it by their incompleteness. Maybe I can put this point into a simple diagram of the four supersensible bodies/organizations, which can manifest through the laws working within, the so called four elements and the **fifth principle, "quinta essentia":**

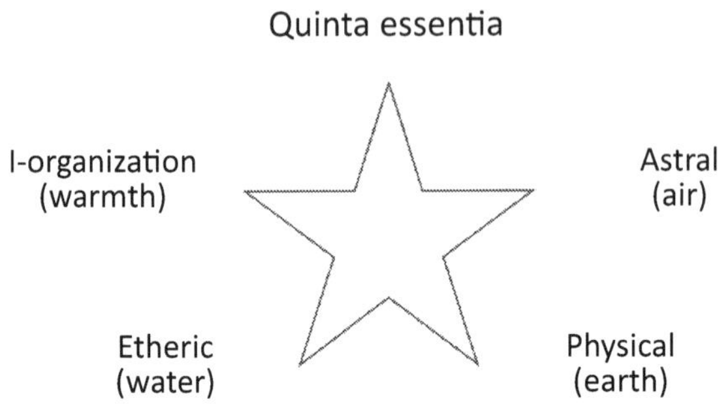

Quinta essentia

I-organization
(warmth)

Astral
(air)

Etheric
(water)

Physical
(earth)

Fig 4.1 Four elements and the fifth principle: Quinta essentia
(out of body manifestation of the etheric, astral and 'I' forces)

Here we have what, in ancient times, were called the four elements, or nowadays, the three aggregate states of matter plus warmth, through which the supersensible bodies can direct our living, our soul and spirit-carrying physical body. This is possible through the laws working within the solid, the liquid, the airy form of matter and warmth. These laws permit our supersensible organizations manifesting in and directing the fourfold appearance of matter. The materialistic view is that matter itself is intelligent and is the producer of everything 'by accident.' From a spiritual point of view, thinking, laws and intelligence have their own spiritual reality, radiating out from spiritual beings and are working **in** matter. It is possible to think spirit in matter, spirit out of matter and also how spirit can transform matter. This is the core of Christian spirituality. That is the difference between the world views. Materialism is monistic and so is anthroposophy, but in another way.

Each of our four bodies—physical, etheric, astral and I-organization—is 'intelligent' and is working with different systems of laws and organizing parts and functions of our physical body, which is not only solid, but also liquid, airy and warm. There is a system of laws manifesting within the solid matter which gives me my individual shape and form. My etheric body can manifest within the physical body through the hydrodynamic laws which are directing my liquids and blood circulation. The astral body needs the aerodynamic laws to manifest within the physical body and allow breathing, voice, movement, language. The I-organization needs the thermodynamic laws, organizing and regulating its warmth states. Warmth itself is immaterial—it is the bridge between spirit and matter. It is the regulating and transforming quality on which the appearance of matter depends. If you put enough heat on something, it will immediately transform and go from one aggregate state into the next, such as ice to boiling water.

The quintessential is that etheric forces are liberated from the body, according to the stage of growing up and aging process. The more you age, the less etheric forces your body has, and therefore we don't look so 'fresh' anymore! It's obvious when these forces leave us. The baby has them, and we lose them! Similarly, our astral forces also gradually leave the body, releasing our feelings. When the I-organization leaves gradually during the growing and aging process of our body, our will is released. The quintessential, fifth principle is what distills out of the body as pure, self-directed laws, acting as our thinking, feeling and willpower. Once released, all these are working out of matter. And that is what makes us incomplete by nature. Animals cannot self-direct these forces as they age. Therefore animals are directed by nature, as long as they are healthy. Once they start to be unhealthy, they are digested by the ecological balance and die. Human beings live their lifelong in health and illness individually, with the double orientation of these forces, embodied and directed by nature and, when out of the body, more or less well self-directed.

Therefore, we need, through our education and self-education, to strive toward a certain fulfillment of humanity as completely as possible in each lifetime. The younger we are, the less we are self-directed. We depend upon adults because we don't know what we are doing if we just follow the many temptations that life presents. A five-year-old, already addicted to computers, does not know that this addiction is bad for him, but it is an 'illness.' He is severely 'ill' already. Nature does not protect us against failure. Nature makes us only one third ready. From Rudolf Steiner, we learn from his book, *The Philosophy of Freedom*:

Nature makes out of us a natural being.

Society makes us an adapted, well-conditioned being that follows instructions, keeping the rules and laws.

The human being can only make a free human being out of himself.[41]

If you think that you are not 'ill by nature,' then I ask you, "Why do you need to learn what to eat, how and when to sleep, how to communicate?" Humans are not guided well by their natural instincts. They are not, by nature, healthy. Even the instincts for food and sleep have to be educated through culture. Only culture and learning processes make us into healthy human beings. We are as healthy as we can attain autonomy on all levels of our existence. The more ill we are, the more we depend upon help and support. If we only adapt to given laws and instructions, if we do not develop the capacity of self-guidance, we fail our humanity. The human being can only make a free human being out of its own self. I cannot force you to become a human being, even if I imprison you, put you on drugs or do whatever I want. I cannot create a free human being out of the 'other' if the 'other' does not want to be. It is not possible. We have to tread this path toward our humanity on our own. Freedom is the single point out of which we have to make the decision of what we

---

41 Steiner, R. (1894/1995). *Intuitive thinking as a spiritual path* (M. Lipson, trans., centennial ed.) [GA 4, chapter 9]. Hudson, NY: Anthroposophic Press.

truly want. And that is the initiation moment. We become healthy through initiation, through our spiritual path. Thank you for asking this question.

Question—*Is it a spiritual reason why animals, not humans, are perfect?*

Yes, it is. There is an ongoing dialogue about what is typical of animals and what is human, as both humans and animals are vertebrates. What is typical of the physical body of an animal? It is perfect. What is typical of the human physical body? It remains embryological. For example, when you compare the embryological development of the human hand with the embryological development of a bird, a tiger, of whatever vertebrate, then you can see that all the vertebrate animals, in their early stages of the embryological development, have a hand like a human hand. However, at a certain period of their development, they lose the human form. It is particularly touching to see this in the wings of a bird. I refer you to a book I co-published, *Education: Health for Life*,[42] in which you can find illustrations of that. In the beginning, the bird's wings start like a human hand. Next, degeneration takes place, and at the end, you have a 'crippled hand' which the bird uses for flying and nothing else. That is specialization. Animals are by nature specialized. It is the astral body which gives specialization and utmost differentiation.

Human beings have an I-organization. Animals cannot incorporate an individual I-organization, because they are specialized in groups. Dogs or birds behave doglike or birdlike out of immense wisdom. The astral body comes here to its highest manifestation. Therefore Rudolf Steiner explains how the animals are directed by a 'group-I,' which

---

42 Glöckler, M., Langhammer, S. & Wiechert, C. (2006). *Education: Health for life*. Dornach, CH: Anthroposophic Medicine Foundation & Medical Section of the Goetheanum.

lives within their warmth, but cannot individualize them into a being which reaches autonomy and could transform itself. What could the 'I' do in a tiger's body? It could not do anything, because the tiger is wise by nature. The 'I' would have no chance for self-consciousness or self-direction (such as transforming itself so it could have the attributes of a mouse or whatever!). No. If the 'I' were in a complete body, which is not perfect by nature, then it cannot transform. It cannot use the fifth principle we just spoke about in an individual way. But whole groups of animals with their 'group-I' have a certain career in this evolution. They develop, appear and disappear. Each individual human being, however, is its own species. Each human is specific. When humans join various 'isms,' they can become driven by collective emotions and can lose their individual guidance and leadership. They are 'animalizing' by serving group spirits, group emotions, making their own 'I' dependent upon and guided by others. I hope this answer has helped to understand the difference.

Question—relating to Steiner's lecture *Truth, Beauty and Goodness*[43]

In Rudolf Steiner's work we often encounter apparent contradictions. That is especially so for such integrating concepts as truth, beauty and goodness. In Steiner's educational lectures we can also find apparent contradictions, such as the concepts of imitation, authority and freedom, which are inter-connected in a complex metamorphosis throughout the learning processes within the first three seven-year periods. In my contribution I did not follow Steiner's lecture about *Truth, Beauty and Goodness*. It was my goal to show how these ideals are expressions of our supersensible bodies, existentially rooted within them.

---

43 Steiner, R. (1923/1986). *Truth, beauty and goodness* [GA 220]. Spring Valley, NY: St. George Publications.

Truth can be reached only by thinking and is therefore 'at home' in our etheric (which is our truth and our health body) in which everything is 'just right,' provided it works.

Beauty comes to our self-experience through our feelings, which are 'at home' in our astral nature. We are still reflecting and researching what, in an academic sense, is objectively beautiful. Yesterday afternoon, in our artistic work with Van James, we contemplated ideals of proportion and completeness by drawing mandalas. We attempt to understand the mystery of the completeness of feelings where all feelings are in harmony. If you learn to play an instrument, then you train day by day to get your tones, from the not so beautiful into the more beautiful. We develop a sense for beauty. I know of an opera star, who, after her performance, in spite of receiving a huge applause, was in tears behind the curtain because she had missed just one note! Access to beauty is through the arts and our differentiated feelings. The astral body is our body of beauty. If the feeling life is underdeveloped, the sense of beauty is badly educated, suppressed and brought to silence; then the negative feelings become strong, destructive desires are coming up. When we want to re-socialize criminals, we need to teach them beauty. They need artistic training and therapy. There are some examples from Japan of therapeutic work with young criminals. They had no 'tools' for beauty in their lives, so they had to learn wise texts and beautiful words by heart. That brought them calmness and re-enlivened empathy.

Goodness: How can I find the good? Can I think the good? No, it is not good when I only think it. Can I feel the good? Yes, but it is only within the world if I do it. We can only train and do the good. It depends upon our I-related 'good will,' serving the needs of the physical plane and the humans around us. That is meaningful, because we can only do the good in the physical. We need a physical body on earth in order to do the good that is obvious. And the physical body is in need of the experience 'that the world is good' in in order to develop healthily. But the good comes only in the world through humans who are doing it.

In Steiner's lecture about *Truth, Beauty and Goodness*, he is developing another aspect. He addresses the question of how we may educate the supersensible bodies through cultivating the feelings:

...The divine nature of our physical body comes from the past and gives us the feeling of truth; our etheric body lives in the present and gives us the sense for beauty. Finally, our astral body prepares for the future, giving us a sense for the good.

The divine, spiritual world, in which the child existed before birth, is the world of truth in the Rosicrucian sense, 'From God we are born.' Through the divine spiritual world, we derive our feeling for truth, our entire connection with the world, and we feel that our existence is justified. Crucially, Rudolf Steiner speaks of a feeling for truth as a remembering of our pre-birth existence:

...The feeling for truth is related to and connected with the general feeling that we have a physical body, originated and spiritually pre-formed as the laws of my physical body in the spiritual world. If we develop sense and feeling for truth, we feel connected and justified within our physical body.

...The feeling within the ether body is grounded through the experience of beauty. ... If we learn to feel the beauty of life and through the arts, which bring spiritual realities in a picture form on earth, we develop a healthy feeling for our etheric body. This body is connected with us in the time directly before birth and carries us through life until death.

...Without feeling the good, we would lose empathy and love for others and their needs. Our astral body would degenerate. By feeling enthusiasm for the good, we empower our astral body and feel

its divine nature, which gives us the consciousness for our path of development toward the future, beyond the threshold of death.

...When a human being is filled with such goodness toward others that they are not confined to their own self-interest and conscious only of what is living within their own being, ...then this goodness can lead the soul into the qualities, nature and experiences of others. It embraces innumerable forces of the soul; and these forces are of such a nature that they actually instill into the human being elements with which they were wholly permeated only in pre-earthly existence. Through the sense of beauty, they link themselves, by means of a picture, to the spirit they had left because of their descent to earthly existence. A truly good person links this earthly life to pre-earthly existence. A good person is one who can bear their own soul over into the soul of another. Upon this all true morality depends, and without morality no true social order among earthly humanity can be maintained.

... Just as the sense of Truth manifests in a human being's right relation to the physical body; just as a warm enthusiasm for Beauty expresses itself in the etheric body, so does Goodness live in the astral body. And the astral body cannot be healthy or maintain its true position in the world if the human being is not able to permeate it with forces proceeding from Goodness.

The aspect Rudolf Steiner is pointing out within this lecture is oriented toward to our relationship with the spiritual world, out of which we came, from which we live, and into which we return.

My intention throughout our morning lectures was to show how the three ideals can become accessible for the educational process within the first three seven-year periods. Through our materialistic culture we are surrounded by a lot of untruthfulness, ugliness and evil. We need an education which helps to reconnect out of our free will with these Ideals. We think with our etheric body, and, through training clear thinking and observation, we meet truth. We feel with our astral body and, through training our differentiated feeling capacities, we learn to experience beauty. We do the good out of our free will if we learn to participate in a helpful way within our physical life circumstances.

I hope that the preceding extracts from Rudolf Steiner's lecture help to clarify your question.

Fifth Principle and the Higher Self

We can strive for the elevated ideals of Truth, Beauty and Goodness through our fifth principle of thinking, feeling and willing. Through daily practice we can strive to become a bit more truthful, to develop our sense for beauty, and to learn more about what is really good for us, for me and for the planet. We know much more about the good than we can do. As an example, suppose we try to be consequential with the business of recycling? When I am at home, I have seven different boxes: one for plastic, wood, metals and so on. When I am traveling and I can't find such boxes, then I feel I am not doing the good, but rather I am being wasteful. We approach the good, but to be consistently successful on the level of action, our 'I' has to work hard. It does not help to just think or feel, "Oh, how exciting, there are recycling boxes!" but we have to actually use them! The physical body is required to make it happen. If momentum is not given to your 'I am,' then you cannot carry out actions, even if you have a wonderful physical body willing to do it. The 'I' is more than only will. The 'I' is our higher self, which is not incarnated.

We have physical, etheric, astral and I-organization which give us, through their laws, the fifth principle, which is like a spiritual vessel for my higher self to approach my thoughts, my feelings and my will, depending how 'attractive' they are for it. Thoughts, feelings and will can make all the plans and they know when I do wrong or right. I can

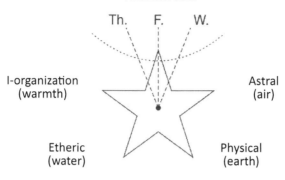

TRUTH   BEAUTY   GOODNESS
HIGHER SELF

Th.   F.   W.

I-organization
(warmth)

Astral
(air)

Etheric
(water)

Physical
(earth)

Fig 4.2 Truth, Beauty and Goodness,
the Fifth Principle and the Higher Self

access my higher self through my thoughts, feelings and my goodwill. I share my higher self with all humanity. My I-organization makes me specifically only me. To think, 'I am me,' occurs usually around three years of age when, for the first time, I begin to make contact with my true higher self. It is a spiritual act. By thinking, 'I am me,' I touch my higher self in thoughts. We can all relate to this 'I am me' experience. No one is jealous that another person says 'I am' about themselves. There is a natural altruism. We are all humans. This is really what makes us a global family. Through this fine thinking capacity I can touch within the etheric the true, purely spiritual entity living as the higher self in the etheric world. We can feel that and we can connect with it in our will. Finally we can even say, as expressed by poets,[44] "Not me, but the higher within me":

---

44 "I am not I" (*Yo no soy yo*) from, Jiménez, J.R. (1973). *Lorca and Jimenez: Selected poems* (R. Bly, trans.). Boston, MA: Beacon Press.

I am not I.
I am this one,
walking beside me whom I do not see,
whom at times I manage to visit
and whom at other times I forget;
Who remains calm and silent while I talk,
and forgives gently when I hate.
who walks where I am not,
who will remain standing when I die.

Poets sense this reality, that we are spiritual beings on a journey to find an individual access to our true spiritual origin and that we are two, one embodied and one out of body. The meaning of one incarnation is to learn and understand more about this access and why we are individuals. Our destiny, with all its pain and peril, makes us very specific individuals.

In all esoteric traditions and deep religious traditions such as Christianity, it is spoken about the first and second birth and the first and second death. The first birth is clear: I incarnate into my physical body and my mother gives me birth. There are other 'births.' Around three years of age, I initiate not only my 'I' consciousness when I think, 'I am.' With nine years of age, which Steiner calls the 'nine year old Rubicon,'[45] for the first time, I feel what it means to be alone and to have this individual 'I am,' which can be painful. At age sixteen, sometimes earlier or later, is another birth, when we first experience that 'I am responsible for me and for others. I am responsible for what I think, what I feel, what I do. I am responsible for my will.' For the first time we really wake up in our will and then we are truly adolescent, with high idealism and lots of plans. Rudolf Steiner names these

---

45 Steiner, R. (1922/1986). *Soul economy and Waldorf education* [GA303, lecture 10]. Spring Valley, NY: Anthroposophic Press.

three births the 'preliminary I am.' We learn about our 'I am' through our development and we need guidance by our teachers. How we manage to find ourselves depends upon our environment and how we are brought up.

Then comes a fourth birth (mostly the earliest is around twenty-three years), when we start to question, 'Is this really me? Is this really what I want to do? Did I take the right subject? Am I with the right partner? Is this really the life I want to live?' Sometimes it appears as a deep crisis, sometimes it is just an ongoing question until we find our answer. Then we initiate our true own, self-directed life. That is the initiation moment, the zero moment, in which life is complete in regards to the 'I am' awareness. It's the fourth decisive 'I am' awareness step of human development. We feel totally free from our past, feel totally free in regard to what we want to become and that we can make our individual judgment and decision of what we want to do.

When we go through this point, we become really adult. Not all grownups are 'adult.' Adulthood is a decision; it is autonomy and self-guidance toward the good, the beautiful and the honest and true choice for our life. We come under the guidance of our higher self and of the three leading stars.

Yesterday I said we can access truth and beauty from this side of the threshold, but for goodness we need to transcend. However, all three—truth, beauty and goodness—in their completeness, are really beyond the threshold. They are the faculties of our higher self.

The Holy Trinity of Father, Son and Holy Ghost: The Higher Self

God is our higher self. The spirit of humanity is true, beautiful and good. The Father (Lord, in Christian terminology) is good. The Son radiates beauty of life, of understanding its nature, including death, and is the teacher and lord of our soul. Christ came to save the soul, not the spirit. Our soul is with the individual human being and the Son gives beauty for life. The Holy Spirit is truth. The Holy Trinity has its vessel in and contact with the higher self. That, I think, is the highest meaning or riddle of this initiation moment, when we realize that Christ sacrificed Himself to humanity in order to give us the possibility to strive for an individual access to the higher self, to the 'Christ within me.' If we accept this sacrifice, He is really with us. His sacrifice is there for everyone, independent of our acceptance or not, but our acceptance makes it conscious for us. If acceptance of this higher self-sacrifice becomes conscious, then truth, beauty and goodness become more of a reality in our lives. We have a conscious access to these three and can receive the strength of this divine radiation into our will, into our I-organization. We can think in a way which gives completeness and healing in our work as teachers, so we can give each child what each child needs, by bringing our quintessential thinking and feeling and willing into the service of others. Once we no longer need these forces for looking after ourselves, then we can use them to help others to make their journey. That is the essence of Waldorf education.

When Rudolf Steiner founded the first Waldorf School, he said, "We start now with an education which is not built on egoism. ..."[46] It is an altruistic education. Steiner then told the doctors that medicine is the most beautiful pathway to understand altruism. Some months before Steiner laid the foundation stone for the first Goetheanum in 1913, he gave lectures about Christ in the etheric.[47] Christ has a school in which one thing will be learned, and that is selflessness. Selflessness is a beautiful word, particularly in English, because it starts with *self*. It's very powerful. Without self, we cannot become self-less. It means

---

46 Steiner, R. (1919/1996). *The foundations of human experience* (R.F. Lathe, trans.) [GA 293, lecture 7, p. 123]. Great Barrington, MA: Anthroposophic Press.
47 Steiner, R. (1910-17/1983). *The reappearance of Christ in the etheric*. Spring Valley, NY: Anthroposophic Press.

that first we need to establish a strong self so that, when we cross the threshold, the zero point, we are so strong in our self that we can look back at ourselves and can question, "Is this really what I want? Is it really what I want to do with my life?" Upon reaching this point, I am not me, but I am the onlooker, who looks from the outside. I wake up and I know that I am a spiritual being and my body and soul forces are my 'tools.' I have found my true being's goal, my anchor. I then experience true freedom of everything.

Only then, when we really feel free can we make a decision to look after others and become self-less. Selflessness does not mean to lose our self or to become a victim or sacrifice. It is the highest power of fulfillment of the self. Reaching out to the higher self as the fulfillment of my becoming, I will not miss anything when I am looking out for the needs of my students, patients, banking customers, or whatever other work I am doing. Rudolf Steiner gave a prayer for those who are in despair, in extreme loneliness, depressed so that they have lost contact with the spiritual world. One can pray for such people to help them connect with their angel. Each angel of each human being lives in the realm of thinking. We can think these concepts. Our angels are living in these concepts of truth, beauty and goodness. We all have this in the angel aura in our spiritual guidance. When we disconnect and don't feel this anymore, then others can connect for us. We can do this for students who have committed suicide or are in danger to do so. With our own human thinking, feeling and willing, we can give good forces to our angel or angel of another person. I contribute this verse from Rudolf Steiner to our conference, because it is about these three ideals. The first is for ourselves when we are in danger, and the second version is what we may speak for another:

> 1. You, spirit of my life's protective companion,
> May you be goodness of heart in my willing,
> May you be human love in my feeling,
> May you be the light of truth in my thinking.

2. You, spirit of (person's name) life's protective companion,
May you be goodness of heart in (person's name) willing,
May you be human love in (person's name) feeling,
May you be the light of truth in (person's name) thinking.

We can understand this verse in the framework of our conference theme. We need the courage to say what we think, to express our concerns, and then to listen to possible answers. Then we can keep going on the pathway toward truth, beauty and goodness. When we do not find answers, we disconnect and we need help, which this verse can give. I would like to close with the thought that with the good there is always the evil on the other side. In our normal life, we would not know what is good without there also being evil. Without the ugly, we would not know beauty and without lies and untruthfulness and doubts, we would not know what truth is. The normal use of the words truth, beauty and good is not what we have talked about in our Conference. The normal usage of the words is what happens before the threshold, where we need life's contradictions in order to wake up to our own free judgments and decision making. True goodness, beauty and truth are part of an all-embracing love which drives our evolution and humanity. Integrated into this divine love are contradictions, tensions and developmental possibilities. Love is really the context in which the true Truth, Beauty and Goodness have their place. On the highest level we have a divine picture of the human being in thinking, feeling and willing. The 'I,' which is pure love, has to direct and use these forces in the best way.

With that thought, I say farewell, and I thank you very much.

Dr Rudolf Steiner (1861–1925)

Rudolf Steiner was a philosopher, scientist, and initiator of anthroposophy (the study of human wisdom) and many other initiatives. He established various practical endeavors whereby over 10,000 institutions and initiatives have been founded, including: biodynamic agriculture, Waldorf education and parenting; anthroposophical extended medicine, pharmaceuticals, nutrition, therapeutic (curative) education and communities, social therapy, psychotherapy; economics and banking; architecture, visual and performing arts, eurythmy and natural science.

Dr Eugen Kolisko (1893–1939)

Eugen Kolisko, an Austrian physician, specialized in preventative medicine and worked closely with Rudolf Steiner. He extended health practices consistent with the age-specific learning process of body, soul and spirit in kindergarten and school-age children. As the first school doctor and chemistry teacher in the first Waldorf School in Stuttgart, he worked closely with teachers and students to better understand learning processes and healthy ways of living. He left an important legacy: collaboration of teachers, doctors, therapists, and parents to support the healthy development of children.

The first Kolisko Conference took place in 1989, Stuttgart, honoring the fiftieth anniversary of the lifework of Dr Eugen Kolisko in the form of an international gathering of physicians and teachers. Kolisko Conferences have since become a platform for promoting education as preventative medicine. Kolisko Conferences took place in 1992 (Austria), 1994 (UK), 1998 (USA), 2002 (Finland), and in 2006 in nine countries (India, South Africa, Philippines, Ukraine, Australia, Mexico, Sweden, France and Taiwan). In France it was hosted in the UNESCO-Hall in Paris, which was also provided as the venue for a Waldorf exhibition and forum to discuss World Education and Health. Since then, Kolisko Conferences have also been held in other locations, including Hawai'i and New Zealand (2010), Taiwan (2013) and Malaysia (2015).

Made in the USA
Middletown, DE
03 July 2025

77725414R00046